Contents

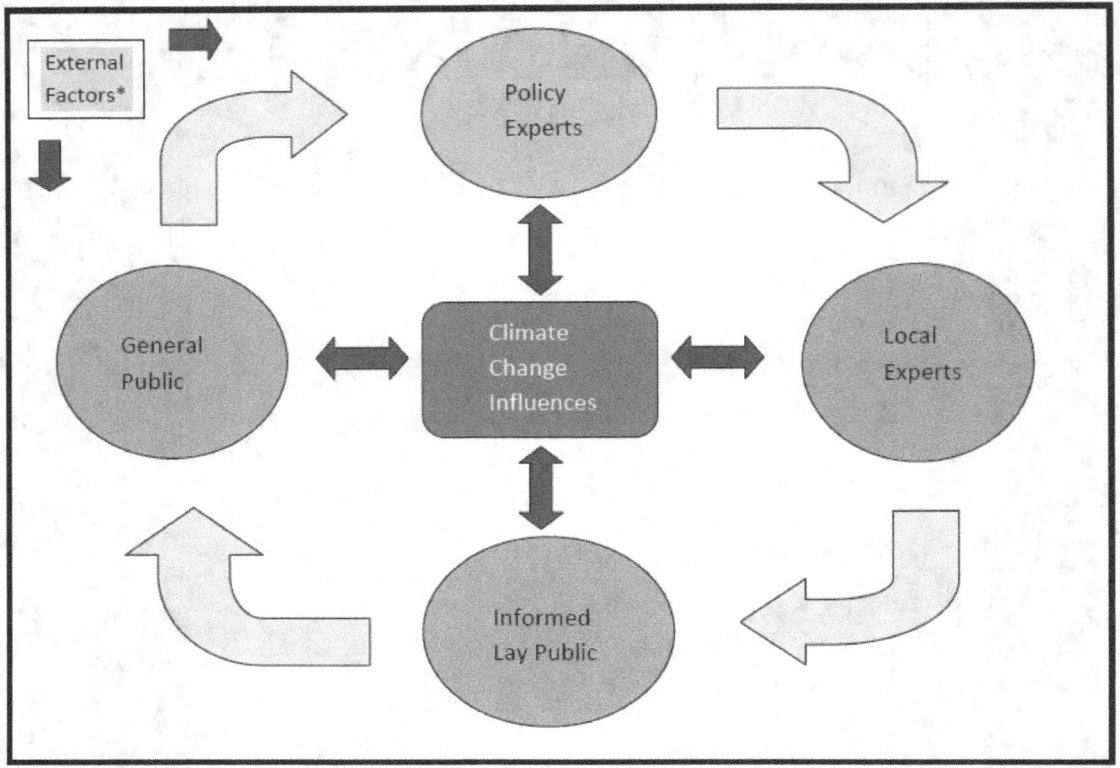

Figure 1—Conceptual framework of stakeholders. *External factors are Congress, fire science, etc.

A Qualitative and Quantitative Analysis of Risk Perception and Treatment Options as Related to Wildfires in the USDA FS Region 3 National Forests

Ingrid M. Martin,
Wade E. Martin,
Carol B. Raish

United States Department of Agriculture

Forest Service
Rocky Mountain Research Station

General Technical Report RMRS-GTR-260

September 2011

ABSTRACT

As the incidence of devastating fires rises, managing the risk posed by these fires has become critical. This report provides important information to examine the ways that different groups or disaster subcultures develop the mentalities or perceived realities that affect their views and responses concerning risk and disaster preparedness. Fire risk beliefs and attitudes of individuals and groups from four geographic areas in the Southwest (U.S. Department of Agriculture, Forest Service, Region 3, Arizona and New Mexico) surrounding the Kaibab, Tonto, Santa Fe, and Lincoln National Forests are presented. Using both quantitative and qualitative methods, we collected information from three distinct groups: general public, informed lay public, and local experts. In addition, personal interviews were conducted with a group of policy experts in the science of wildfires and climate change. A primary finding indicates that all of the groups that we interviewed expressed a strong desire for land managers to manage the public lands proactively in order to reduce the risk of catastrophic wildfire. However, respondents expressed different preferences regarding the management approach that should be used. One important observation was that respondents in each of the three distinct respondent groups prioritized their preferred means of communication differently.

Keywords: wildfire, risk perceptions, risk communication, risk mitigation, disaster subcultures, attitudes, beliefs, prescribed fire

AUTHORS

Ingrid M. Martin, Department of Marketing, California State University, Long Beach, and Integrated Resource Solutions, LLC, imartin@csulb.edu.

Wade E. Martin, Department of Economics, California State University, Long Beach, and Integrated Resource Solutions LLC, wmartin@csulb.edu.

Carol B. Raish, Rocky Mountain Research Station, U.S. Department of Agriculture, Forest Service, Albuquerque, New Mexico, craish@fs.fed.us.

ACKNOWLEDGMENTS

We thank Pam Jakes and Stacey Menzel Baker for their helpful comments. This research was supported, in part, by funds provided by the Rocky Mountain Research Station, Forest Service, U.S. Department of Agriculture. RJVA 07-JV-11221602-176.

1.0 Introduction

Various factors have emerged to increase risk of catastrophic wildfires in our National Forests. Years of suppression of natural fires, an increase in human populations living in and around the forests, changes in climate such as prolonged droughts, and beetle infestations are just some of those factors. With the rising occurrence of devastating fires, managing risk has become critical. This report provides background information to examine the ways in which different groups or disaster subcultures[1] develop the mentalities or perceived realities that affect their views and responses concerning risk and disaster preparedness. Fire risk beliefs and attitudes of individuals and groups from four geographic areas in the Southwest (U.S. Forest Service, Region 3, Arizona and New Mexico) surrounding the Kaibab, Tonto, Santa Fe, and Lincoln National Forests (NF) are presented. Our research shows differing views and attitudes among: local experts, involved public, and general public. In addition, we investigate the policies that guide public land management decisions concerning wildfire using a set of interviews with experts from various agencies at the national level (figure 1).

We explore stakeholder groups' views on the role of fire and on wildfire risk and vulnerability. Pursuing the topic of risk in greater detail, we examine acceptable levels of risk and what factors motivate people to take actions to mitigate risk on their property and in their community. Information concerning assignment of responsibility for risk mitigation actions forms another part of the investigation.

We also present detailed discussions concerning preferred forest treatment options to reduce the risk of wildfire on public lands surrounding communities and which factors facilitate treatment implementation. Trust levels varied across the geographic areas, as well as among individuals within each area, but general patterns were apparent. In addition to historic and contemporary trust issues, we explore the effects of agency communication and education programs on trust and on public perceptions of risk. We compare trust levels, agency communication efforts, and educational programs across the four geographic areas. These topics are examined in the context of both historic and contemporary relationships and trust that individuals and communities place in relevant Government agencies, primarily in the U.S. Forest Service (FS) (figure 1).

---

[1] Disaster subcultures refers to a cultural adaptation in coping with recurrent threats and the cultural defense used by a group to adapt to cognitive, behavioral, individual and collective behaviors used by people in response to a disaster that has struck or has the potential to strike in the future (Tierney and others 2001).

1.1 Research Process

In this study, we review and evaluate community and individual knowledge, beliefs, attitudes, preferences, and practices concerning fire and fuels management in southwestern forest, woodland, and grassland ecosystems in both historic and contemporary contexts. Published and archival information on indigenous and traditional burning practices formed the historic background for the research conducted with adjacent communities and user groups on NFs and Grasslands in the FS Southwestern Region (Region 3). Information was collected by means of focus groups and one-on-one interviews with locally knowledgeable individuals and the involved public from four Forests and one Grassland. Successful public communication programs were examined, as well as the public's perceptions of the role of the FS concerning fire and fuels management. This body of issue development research was used to produce a survey instrument to assist us in gathering the desired information across the entire Region.

Although fire is increasingly recommended as a vegetation management tool on both public and private lands, controversy often inhibits its use. Insufficient communication and understanding between land managers and the public contribute to these difficulties. The term "public" refers to a very diverse set of stakeholders that bring an equally diverse set of knowledge, beliefs, attitudes, preferences, and practices regarding fire and fuels management. These stakeholders include the general public, involved lay public, local and regional experts, and national-level policy workers. Understanding the diversity of stakeholder opinions and concerns is critical to efficient and equitable decisionmaking.

Often, managers lack information concerning the public's knowledge, beliefs, attitudes, preferences, and practices regarding fire and fuels management. Managers have inadequate data on the socioeconomic consequences of differing fire management practices to adjacent communities. They lack necessary information on community and user group preferences for fire management and vegetation restoration techniques. In many cases, the public is not sufficiently engaged in the design and implementation of fire and fuels management programs, leading to an incomplete understanding of community desires and concerns by public land managers. This frequently results in a refusal to accept agency initiatives, which hinders program implementation. In the aftermath of the devastating fires of 2000 through 2009 in the Southwest, it is especially important to understand public perceptions and values in the wildland-urban interface (WUI) areas.

In order to design and implement successful, socially acceptable fire and fuels management policies and programs, land managers require an accurate, current body of data on the previously mentioned topics concerning fire. They need adequate information on community and user group preferences for fire management and vegetation restoration techniques, as well as information on the socioeconomic consequences of different fire and incident management techniques. To obtain and make good use of these data, as well as the secondary data collected to support this research, managers must understand the means, methods, and implications of involving the public as partners in the design and implementation of fire and fuels management programs.

We conducted a literature review of published and unpublished archival sources to develop a database concerning fire attitudes and use among historic Native American, traditional Hispanic, and Anglo-American groups in the region. Information was drawn from historic, ethnohistoric, ethnographic, and archeological materials. This body of data served as the background framework to guide our research (see Daniel and others 2007), and it was designed to provide managers with important insights into a potentially useful body of traditional local knowledge and techniques for fire management and use that have been practiced successfully in the area for generations.

In the data collection process, we focus on designing and implementing strategies to gather information on public knowledge, beliefs, attitudes, preferences, and practices relating to fire use and fuels management and to the role of fire in southwestern ecosystems. The public's perceptions about the role of the FS in fire and fuels management, an evaluation of its current role, and information on problems and concerns related to fire and fuels management were also collected. Information was elicited on desired public outcomes from fire and fuels management programs and on possible public responses to different fire and fuels management techniques.

In order to understand how these views may vary with cultural conditioning, residence location, and past experience, as well as to include the varied user groups of the Southwest, we collected data from Native American, Hispanic, and Anglo-American communities. Given the very different groups and their respective stakeholder sub-groups, we developed a strategy to collect broader and more generalizable information using data collection techniques that were suitable for each group. For example, using direct mail surveys was not a feasible approach for the rural Hispanic population in northern New Mexico. Instead, identifying and talking with community leaders was a more effective way to uncover information that enhanced our understanding of what factors lead to public acceptance of hazardous fuels reduction, rehabilitation, and restoration alternatives across varying cultural and user groups.

1.2 Prior Research

In our research on historical published information relating to fire use, management, and attitudes among indigenous and traditional peoples, we examined reviews from various parts of the United States and Canada (Dobyns 1981; Kay 1994; Lewis 1973, 1985; Pyne 1982, 1995; Stewart 1955a, 1955b; Williams 2002). Although they provided an important background, the studies generally did not include the Southwest. To remedy this deficiency, we entered into a cooperative agreement with Quivira Research Associates to conduct a review of the southwestern literature (Condie unpublished paper; Condie and Raish 2003). A review of southwestern unpublished sources, such as archival documents, photographs, and maps, was conducted by consulting historian Thomas Merlan (03-JV-11221611-051). These studies are reported elsewhere (Condie unpublished paper; Condie and Raish 2003).

Studies of community fire issues that are being undertaken by a variety of researchers at both national and regional levels also helped structure research questions for this study. The work of Martin and others (2009) in the Colorado Front Range was used as a comparative base for the work being conducted for this project. The Colorado project by Martin and others (2009) that involves interviewing in multiple communities in Colorado and Oregon, was designed to consider the role of information in the acceptance of various treatment options for fire and fuels management, as well as the impact of experience and knowledge on risk perceptions and risk-mitigating behaviors (see Martin and others 2007, 2008; Martin and others 2008; Martin and others 2008; Martin and others 2009). Their research also examines attitudes, beliefs, and practices concerning various fire and risk management strategies.

1.3 Research Setting, Methods, and Techniques

Information was collected on public knowledge, beliefs, attitudes, preferences, and practices relating to fire use, fuels management, and the perceived role of fire in southwestern ecosystems. The techniques used to gather this information were (1) the development of an historical documentation of fire in the Region, (2) interviews with locally knowledgeable individuals from adjacent communities and user groups, (3) focus group meetings on targeted forests and grasslands throughout the Region for issue and questionnaire development, (4) surveys of forest and grassland users from all forests and grasslands throughout the Region, and (5) interviews with national-level policy experts on fire and climate change.

1.4 Details of the Multi-Phase Research Process

Our research was a multi-phase process taking place in fire-prone communities in New Mexico and Arizona over a four-year period that included two high fire damage seasons (2004 and 2007). The stakeholders that were interviewed were the involved publics in these areas because they were at the forefront of the discussions, research, and/ or governance. The interviews included residents as well as government representatives from local and regional offices, business leaders, volunteer firefighters, and city and county representatives. The population of participants, who were interviewed both through a mail survey and face-to-face, were categorized based on their level and type of involvement with issues related to wildland fire.

The categorization scheme included four groups. The first group was the general public, defined as those individuals living within a 15 mile radius of a NF. Information from this group was obtained via a mail survey (see Appendix B). The second group included individuals from the WUI who were identified as the involved lay public (e.g., Homeowner's Association [HOA] participants, recreationists, representatives from environmental groups, and extractive user groups). Information from this group was obtained using a focus group format. The third group was made up of individuals who were primarily responsible for implementing wildland fire policy such as local firefighters or local fire management officers (FMO). These individuals were identified as local experts. The fourth group included those whose primary responsibility was to establish guidelines and policy direction for implementation of wildland fire policy, such as members of State and Private Forests and National Wildfire Coordinating Group (Bureau of Indian Affairs [BIA], Bureau of Land Management [BLM], National Park Service [NPS], USDA FS, Federal Emergency Management Agency [FEMA], National Association of State Foresters [NASF], etc.) as well as experts on climate change and wildfires. These individuals were identified as policy experts. Individual interviews were conducted with the latter two groups.

The local experts and involved lay public were asked the same set of questions with some customizing to fit each group. We used QSR, a qualitative data analysis program, to aid in analyzing the results of the interviews. The second part of the process was a mail survey that was sent to a random sample of the general public (residents in New Mexico and Arizona), and the response rate was 25.1%.[2] This group lives within 15 miles of a NF, and its level of actual risk tended to be lower than the involved lay public group because of its proximity to the Forest. The survey results provided information on the general public's beliefs and perceptions of risk from the perspective of a resident that was not directly involved in wildfire issues. Individuals classified as policy experts were identified through a snowball sampling technique and were interviewed either face-to-face or via telephone using a set of specific questions designed to help better understand how policy was developed and communicated within and across agencies. The policy experts were responsible for the development and implementation of policies within and across agencies both in Washington, DC, and across the United States. They were identified as experts in wildfire management and climate change policies based upon their positions as policy advisors and/or decision-makers.

One focus of this report is to discuss the themes that emerged in this research from the perspective of the communities and the (sometimes opposing) perspectives of the various government agencies and businesses. The second focus of this report is to provide the results of the general population survey and to communicate similarities and differences in the results between the two methods. These results are integrated into the discussion of the qualitative analysis with some additional quantitative analysis presented in the Appendix C. The interview guides we used for face-to-face and telephone interviews are found in Appendix A. Discussions were focused around four general topics: (1) the role of fire in the NFs, (2) the risk of catastrophic fires and the reasons why respondents do/do not take action to mitigate that risk, (3) the forest/fuels treatment options available to mitigate risk, and (4) the role of the FS in protecting the forests. We also present an in-depth discussion and analysis of the perspectives of three of the four stakeholder groups. The results and summary of the interviews of the policy experts are presented in Section 9. Our objective in this discussion is to identify where there is potential for communication and education by the FS so as to improve relationships with the stakeholder groups. In the final section of this report, we seek to link the voices of the other three stakeholder groups with the policy experts so that opportunities to improve communication and education can be implemented.

---

[2] We were concerned that the low response rate would result in non-response bias. To check for such bias, we conducted a set of focus group meetings and administered a subset of the survey questions. The results from this survey were treated as a hold-out sample and analyzed separately following Dillman (2000). A set of t-tests confirmed that there were no significant differences between the two groups (Martin and others 2009).

2.0 The Role of Fire

For many years, fires were seen as a threat to the forests and the natural resources derived from them and, therefore, as something to be prevented. Smokey Bear and his well-known "Only You Can Prevent Forest Fires" message, the longest running public service campaign in the United States, were created in 1944 in response to a national fear of the threat that fire posed to the lumber industry, which was critical to supporting the war effort of the time. Since then, the perception of fire and the contribution of forest fire suppression to the preservation of forest resources appear to have come full circle.

In the general public survey, respondents said they believed that they were moderately well-informed and motivated to learn more about the connection among wildfire risks, the role of fire, and defensible space actions (table 1). This was consistent in each of the four locations. In addition, respondents said they felt that information about wildfires was moderately relevant to them, providing an opportunity to further inform residents.

Keeping in mind that the interviews and focus groups were conducted with involved lay people as well as local and regional policy experts, we did not assess respondents' levels of knowledge and motivation to learn more about fires. Overall, we found that Region 3 stakeholders expressed a respect for forest fires as "part of the natural life of the forest." Further, many said they view forest fires as playing an important role in contributing to the health of the forest, with some stating that forest fires are a "[natural] cleanser of our ecosystem" and others expressing that fires provide "important nutrients back into the soil." As such, there appeared to be strong support for allowing natural fire cycles to take place rather than suppressing them, as was previously done. There was a wide-ranging view that fires should be allowed as part of "the natural thinning [of the forest] and not trying to rush out there and fight [them]." Suppressing fire was often seen as going against nature. As an HOA representative on the Tonto expressed, "Historically, the forests...have been cleared naturally by forest fires."

Interviewees largely shared the opinion that a history of fire suppression is one of the primary contributors to the current condition of the NFs, including the sharp increase in forest density, the widespread bark beetle infestation that is killing trees, and, ultimately, the rise in fuel loading that has led to a greater risk of catastrophic fires. The increase in catastrophic fires is widely regarded as the consequence of all the years of putting out every fire there was instead of allowing it or looking at it as part of the natural ecosystem. However, despite a general disagreement with suppression as a policy for managing the forest, suppression was considered necessary at some level due to the perceived risk of catastrophic fires under existing forest conditions. As expressed by a representative from the Arizona Game and Fish Department in Kaibab, fire suppression is necessary "when you've got buildings and [the] public to protect." This is especially the case in areas that are considered WUI, where the threat to lives and property from letting fires burn is perceived to be too high. Under the current conditions, there was significant fear in the population of the devastation a large fire can cause. As one resident and former Fire Chief on the Santa Fe NF expressed, "If we have a catastrophic fire, it's going to kill dozens with widespread destruction."

A closer look at the differences in perspectives by interviewee type showed significant differences in the value they place on fire. Agency and professional forest management staff at the local and regional levels that were interviewed said they valued fire as a natural cleanser for the forest and as a means of controlling fuel loadings. On the other hand, the typical surveyed WUI resident was just as likely to value the aesthetic and practical role that fire plays in contributing to vegetation and grass growth as he/she is to value its role in reducing fuel loadings, contributing to safer conditions in the forest, and contributing to the natural balance of the ecosystem.

An analysis of the perceived role of fire across Forests showed that interviewees on the Santa Fe NF recognize the vital role that fire plays in maintaining the natural balance in the ecosystem. Respondents were twice as likely to cite this as a reason they believe fire is a good and necessary part of the forest as they were to cite any other reason. Other top reasons that residents of the Santa Fe said they believe fire is good are fire's role in the healthy regeneration of grass and vegetation, followed by fire's role in controlling the density of the forest and reducing fuel loadings.

Table 1. How well-informed and motivated are WUI residents?

Knowledge	Overall mean (SD)	Arizona		New Mexico	
		northern region	southern region	northern region	southern region
How well-informed	4.77 (1.52)	4.61 (1.46)	4.75 (1.56)	4.84 (1.55)	4.96 (1.56)
How relevant is information	4.65 (1.58)	4.69 (1.48)	4.38 (1.68)	4.79 (1.62)	4.71 (1.54)
How motivated to learn	4.78 (1.68)	4.76 (1.68)	4.38 (1.71)	4.93 (1.64)	5.15 (1.66)
Sample size	502	152	119	141	90

1 = not at all informed/motivated to 7 = very well informed/motivated

These strong opinions about the role of fire were mirrored when looking at state-level differences in perceptions of policy (table 2). Where interviewees in New Mexico tended to express a strong appreciation of fire for its role in the natural balance of the ecosystem, controlling forest density and fuel levels, and contributing to healthy vegetation re-growth, Arizona interviewees showed no strong opinion. Respondents were just as likely to value those attributes as they were to value fire's role in creating meadows and helping to create good habitat for wildlife. These differences could be attributed to the different cultures as well as to the fire history of the areas, among other factors. The results of the survey of the general public revealed that residents near all four Forests said they believe that "managing naturally ignited fires" is a moderately effective treatment option (M = 4.34, SD = 1.47).

Table 2. Effectiveness ratings of forest treatment options.

Forest treatment options preferences	Overall means (SD)	Arizona		New Mexico	
		northern region	southern region	northern region	southern region
Prescribed fire	4.86 (1.50)	4.81 (1.55)	5.11 (1.19)	4.66 (1.51)	4.90 (1.70)
Managing natural ignited fire	4.34 (1.47)	4.42 (1.44)	4.38 (1.46)	4.20 (1.52)	4.37 (1.52)
Selective thinning (small wood)	5.11 (1.42)	4.85 (1.56)	5.02 (1.34)	5.30 (1.37)	5.33 (1.33)
Selective thinning (large wood)	4.21 (1.73)	4.07 (1.71)	4.31 (1.68)	4.30 (1.75)	4.21 (1.86)
Prescribed fire and thinning small wood	5.18 (1.44)	5.09 (1.54)	5.46 (1.22)	5.15 (1.44)	5.03 (1.52)
Prescribed fire and logging	4.43 (1.74)	4.38 (1.73)	4.75 (1.76)	4.43 (1.63)	4.10 (1.85)
Goats	4.75 (1.69)	4.63 (1.55)	4.49 (1.81)	5.01 (1.67)	4.92 (1.79)
Salvage logging	4.69 (1.78)	4.50 (1.92)	4.67 (1,69)	4.74 (1.74)	4.96 (1.74)
Thin diseased trees	5.55 (1.54)	5.52 (1.64)	5.54 (1.22)	5.61 (1.51)	5.58 (1.48)
Do nothing	2.08 (1.45)	2.41 (1.69)	1.81 (1.24)	1.83 (1.05)	2.32 (1.66)
Sample size	502	152	119	141	90

1 = not at all effective to 7 = very effective

3.0 Perception of Risk

There was a high level of awareness among the residents of Region 3 concerning the threat that wildfires represent to them, to their community, and to the forest, overall. This awareness was largely accompanied by a respect for wildfire as a natural part of living in the forest and, therefore, an understanding that is expressed by many that by choosing to "[live and work] in a heavily wooded forest...risk [of wildfires] is part of our life."

Awareness of the increased risk of catastrophic fires created by current forest conditions and the need to mitigate that risk through treatment was highest among full- and long-time residents of the forest, as well as among people who had recently experienced a catastrophic fire. As the FMO on the Santa Fe NF put it, "These people have had enough scares over the last few years with fires that they've become very smart about fire." Because of their experience, these groups see fire as inevitable and understand that it's not a matter of "if fire comes through, [but] when." They view creating a defensible space around their homes as a priority to mitigate their risk—so much so that New Mexico has a strong defensible space funding program called the 20-Communities Cost Sharing Program, which is funded by the National Fire Plan. The Program is a grant program, administered by the State of New Mexico, that reimburses landowners up to 70% of the cost of clearing hazardous fuels on their land. The success of the 20-Communities Cost Sharing Program has resulted in the program being expanded to over 300 communities in New Mexico.

Risk perceptions were lowest among part-time and seasonal residents, especially those who lived out-of-state. As one resident on the Lincoln NF put it, "summer snowbirds... don't spend a lot of time worrying about fire abatement. It's mostly the permanent residents." Awareness of the risk was low among people who were new to the forest and did not have a good understanding of what the natural state of the Southwest forests should be. According to a Lincoln NF volunteer, "[The forest is] so dense...that it is a disaster waiting to happen."

Residents' perceptions of risk were also driven by their level of knowledge and experience with wildfires. In the general population survey, we asked how much information and experience respondents had concerning wildfires (Appendix C: table 7). We asked how informed they were about wildfire risks, how personally relevant they found information on wildfires to be, and how motivated they were to learn as much as possible about wildfires. We also asked them what type of experience they had with large-scale wildfires, including such aspects as being evacuated and losing homes or structures. Finally, we asked them to report what type of information they had been exposed to over the last year related to wildfires. Possible sources of information were Federal, State, and local agencies; media reports; neighbors; environmental organizations; and fire departments.

3.1 Perceived Vulnerability

Many said they view suppression and the removal of fire from the forest as major contributing factors to the forest being overgrown, as fire has not been allowed to play its natural role in removing debris and small trees from the forest. A resident of the Nambe Pueblo in New Mexico discussed the importance of the cultural knowledge of fire as a means to "...clean up the duff and probably also take out a good part of the little seedlings so just the bigger ones live." The fact that this natural thinning of the forest was not taking place was seen by many, including a member of the Firewise Communities in Jemez and on the Santa Fe NF, as "the reason why [the forests are] in such bad shape...because the fuels are so high." These high-density fuel levels were seen as key factors contributing to an increase in catastrophic fires, especially to the devastating crown fires witnessed in many of the area's recent forest fires. While all fires have the potential to cause widespread devastation, there was a perception that crown fires are more destructive and less manageable than ground fires. As one farm owner of Apache descent on the Santa Fe NF stated, "If you can keep [fire] on the ground, you can protect anything on the ground. When this thing starts coming at you from the top, then you're lost...you've lost it."

The Southwest Region had also experienced drier than normal weather in recent years, which was seen as a contributor to the increased risk conditions. As a retired Fire Chief on the Tonto NF stated, "...with the drier weather patterns that have come along, the larger [the] fires that are happening." Dry weather conditions limit the moisture available to the trees, which already compete for water because of the increasingly dense condition of the forest. The lack of moisture creates unhealthy trees and gives rise to an environment suitable for widespread disease in the forest and a rise in the risk of catastrophic fires. Beetle infestation is on the rise, which results in large numbers of dead trees in the forest. As a resident and HOA representative on the Tonto stated, "The way the trees are dying, there's going to be a bigger risk for fire. [Bark beetles] are killing trees and that's just, it makes it 10 times worse. Dead trees go up, you know, it's like pouring gasoline on them." Because of these conditions, people said they feel that any fire has the potential of being a catastrophic fire.

Another factor that increased residents' feelings of vulnerability to catastrophic fire is the perception that the majority of fires that have burned through the Region were caused by humans and were not naturally ignited. One major factor that was seen as contributing to the rise in human-caused fires is that there are more people living in and around the forest than ever before. Further, people are moving into the forests who do not understand them and how to live safely in them given the current conditions. As a County Supervisor in the region of the Tonto NF put it, "We have a lot of people moving into the area that have not lived here before…. They have a tendency to just want to let everything crowd right up against their house. They love their trees!" Another factor that was perceived to increase the feelings of vulnerability is residents not treating their properties, either because, as the County Supervisor near the Tonto NF stated, they "don't understand what the requirement is out here in order to reduce the fuel loadings to where it's manageable" or simply because "they don't want to do it." This perception of vulnerability from untreated land was often attributed to FS land. As an HOA resident near the Tonto NF put it, people feel that even if "everyone has expended a lot of effort to clean their own private property, that doesn't do any good if the fire originates from a horribly overgrown forest…onto the private land." There is strong sentiment that the FS has forsaken its responsibility to reduce fire risks on public land and has instead placed the onus of responsibility on private owners, local governments, and State Forestry.

Analysis of the perception of vulnerability across interviewee type revealed no major differences in the factors associated with a high level of vulnerability between the typical resident and local experts (fire professionals). Both of these groups expressed a strong opinion and concern about the causes of the high level of vulnerability associated with their location, such as their proximity to public lands and neighbors who don't treat their own land. However, resident respondents were much more likely to express a feeling of vulnerability associated with their proximity to FS land. In fact, the average resident respondent was two times more likely to express feeling threatened by their proximity to unmanaged and heavily fuel-laden FS land than they were to express feeling threatened by the condition of their neighbor's property. Local experts, on the other hand, seemed to make no differentiation between the threat caused by unmanaged FS land and neighbors with untreated properties. One interesting point of differentiation between the two groups, however, shows local experts largely attributed to luck that no major catastrophic fire had devastated their area.

A look at differences in the perception of vulnerability across forests showed residents near the Santa Fe NF expressing feelings of vulnerability more so than residents of any other Forest. Factors contributing to this anxiety were a general feeling that it's a matter of time before a major catastrophic fire devastates their area; a feeling that there are more people in the forests, and that this increase in population is contributing to the increase in probability of fire; and a fear of loss of property and lives should a major fire break out. Residents of the Lincoln NF also expressed that the increased population living in the forest contributed to their feelings of vulnerability over the threat of a major fire in their area; however, they did not see loss of life and property as a significant concern. No strong opinion was evident in the Arizona Forests with regard to perception of vulnerability.

In the general population survey, we asked how residents in the WUI felt about their safety, including how vulnerable they believed they and their property were to the potential impact of wildfires (table 3). We also asked them what they believed the perceived likelihood was of a wildfire happening near their property and how severe they would expect that wildfire to be. The low to moderate perceptions of the wildfire vulnerability emerged across all four locations. When asked about their feelings of vulnerability, respondents expressed that they believed that the possibility of wildfires affecting them and their property was moderate. The belief that a catastrophic wildfire could happen near their property was low for southern Arizona and moderate for the other three regions. One distinction that emerged was with the perception of severity of a wildfire if it were to occur. New Mexico and northern Arizona groups said they perceive the severity of a wildfire to be moderately severe, whereas southern Arizona groups perceive the severity to be much less.

It is possible that this was due to the ecology and the topography of the region. According to a local FMO, there is less dense timber country in one part of the southern Arizona region, which tends to be more of a grassy mesquite bosque with a lower fire risk than dense timber country. In addition, according to another fire professional in the Sonoran Desert portions of southern Arizona, that area is not fire-adapted. Fires in this vegetation type cause cacti loss and change the ecosystem to savannah and invasive grasses that make the area more fire prone. Because of these conditions and the proximity of Phoenix's dense population, fire response in the Sonoran Desert is rapid with immediate suppression. It might be for those reasons that the general public in southern

Table 3. Vulnerability, risk, and severity of wildfires.

Perceived vulnerability	Overall mean (SD)	Arizona		New Mexico	
		northern region	southern region	northern region	southern region
How vulnerable are you?[a]	3.33 (1.96)	3.66 (1.95)	2.68 (1.75)	3.45 (2.03)	3.49 (2.01)
How vulnerable is your home?[a]	3.24 (2.05)	3.58 (2.05)	2.56 (1.91)	3.37 (2.13)	3.44 (1.99)
Likelihood of wildfire[b]	3.51 (2.69)	4.13 (2.72)	2.62 (2.62)	3.67 (2.64)	3.36 (2.58)
Severity of wildfire[b]	5.02 (3.25)	5.27 (3.15)	3.91 (2.94)	5.42 (3.43)	5.38 (3.33)
Sample size	502	152	119	141	90

1 = not at all vulnerable/likely/severe to 7 = very vulnerable/likely/severe
[a] These measures are based upon a 7-point scale.
[b] These measures are based upon a 0 to 10 rating.

Arizona believed the impact of wildfire in the next couple of years would be significantly lower than did members of the general public in the other three regions.

3.2 Acceptable Level of Risk

While residents expressed that they understand and are willing to accept some level of risk from living in the forest, it is important for land managers to understand that not all risk is acceptable. Self-imposed risk, the risk residents take on by choosing to live in the forest, is acceptable; the risk imposed on them by others is generally not acceptable. An example of this dichotomy comes from a fifth generation resident of the Lincoln NF who said, "I love my trees and I'm going to keep them, and I don't think fire is going to start on my land, but I live near NF land and since the FS isn't taking care of their land they're creating a danger and imposing it on me...homeowners see that as wrong." Other neighbors can also create this risk because of a choice or other limitations that prohibit them from treating their own property. This includes neighbors who own property or land but do not live near the forest full-time and do not maintain it, as one resident near the Lincoln NF stated, "They can care less about clearing out their property or not...because they are not going to live there anyway." Private property issues tend to arise in these types of situations—"Don't tell me what to do on my land!" People, such as a County Representative in the Tonto NF region, said they view ordinances that require people to clean up their properties as the only recourse to deal with this risk because "if your neighbor has got dead trees and so forth on their property right next to you and he's not willing to do anything about it what recourse do you have if you don't have something on the books?"

A form of imposed risk that was somewhat acceptable is the risk that is inherent in treatments such as prescribed fire. While people recognized there is always the risk of a prescribed fire going out of control, they are generally willing to accept that risk since they view it as less risky than doing nothing and increasing the threat of a catastrophic fire. As a NF representative on the Santa Fe NF stated, "Catastrophic fires, wildfires, generally have more of an effect on sites than prescribed fire because they're roaring and going usually when they start burning high density fuel types. And certainly the prescribed fire can be controlled around a site or through sites much more so."

3.3 Why People Take Action

Many factors contributed to motivating people to treat their property and create defensible spaces around their homes. Among these factors was an increased awareness of the threat of and damage caused by catastrophic fires that comes from experience with wildfire. People are more motivated and open to treatment immediately after a fire. This high level of motivation, however, is often not maintained as apathy sets in and as time passes. As a retired Fire Chief on the Tonto NF observed, after a fire "there [is] a great awareness for a short period of time, but then usually, I would say within two months, everybody [is] back to business as usual." The fact that the immediate impact of a fire and the increased feelings of vulnerability seemed to be the strongest factors moving people to action suggests the importance of education and other outreach efforts to raise awareness of the current conditions and what each person can do to mitigate their risk. In other words, using immediate experience as a "teachable moment" can be very effective. However, this requires being prepared to take advantage of that often short two-month window.

Another factor that seemed to motivate people into action is the fact that they generally care about preserving the forest, and not just simply their property. They want to restore the beauty of the forest that has been compromised by the increase in density of trees and fuel loadings. As a resident near the Santa Fe NF stated, "You used to see this beautiful, dense forest and now all [you] see is fuel." There is recognition from many, voiced by a Woods Watch representative on the Kaibab NF, that failure to address the density issue through treatment will result in "nature [taking] care of the problem through the bark beetle infestations and through catastrophic wildfire." The realization that it is possible for land owners to thin out their property and "create that defensible space...in an aesthetic manner" is a motivator because, as one resident of the Santa Fe NF stated, the owner can have the satisfaction of "[having] a piece of land that's defensible [that is] still beautiful." This was important to many who chose to live in the forest.

While these perceptions on why people take action to mitigate their risk of catastrophic fire generally hold true across interviewee type and forest, it is interesting to note the strong perception on the Lincoln NF that personal interest (e.g., the idea that "all of my personal treasures are in my house") was the number one reason why people decide to take action.

In terms of perceptions on why people don't take action, local experts and the involved lay public alike expressed the strong opinion that people near the forest chose to live there because they love to have trees around them, and it is that love that encourages them to resist removing the trees, therefore creating defensible spaces around their homes. A look across Forests for reasons why people chose not to take action also revealed some interesting differences. Representatives interviewed on the Kaibab NF were just as likely to state apathy and lack of awareness as the reasons why people don't take action to mitigate risk. On the Tonto NF, apathy was, by far, the number one reason why people chose not to take action. In fact, a look at perceptions across the two states showed Arizona interviewees sharing the strong opinion that apathy was the number one reason, whereas for the resident New Mexico interviewees, love of trees was the number one reason. This suggests the need for more education and outreach programs in Arizona to raise awareness and prevent apathy from setting in. For New Mexico, programs such as the 20-Communities Cost Sharing Program can be marketed more heavily to encourage both full- and part-time homeowners to put effort into mitigating the fire risk on their property, while also teaching them that they do not have to clear-cut their property in order to make it defensible.

Despite compelling reasons in favor of treatment, significant challenges abound. Not the least among these challenges is the high cost and labor-intensive nature of undertaking various treatment options on one's property. While most "believe [treatment] needs to be done...[some are limited because they either] can't physically...[or they] don't have the money to hire someone to do it," or both. This is especially true for the elderly. The labor-intensive nature of defensible space actions also presents a challenge for the FS, which has limited resources and an increased demand for reporting and administrative duties. People said they perceive the FS as not having the manpower to both apply treatments and meet other duties. As one retired Fire Chief in the Tonto NF stated, "Looking at it very aggressively, you go out there and tell somebody they need to cut down three-quarters of their trees and the first thing they want to do is run you off with a shotgun."

3.4 Individual Risk Mitigation Efforts

To determine how respondents in the general public survey used their knowledge and the information that they had to mitigate wildfire risks on their properties, we asked them to tell us the likelihood of their undertaking 11 defensible space actions[3] (table 4):

1. creating a 30-ft defensible space around your home,

2. planting fire-resistant plants around your home,

3. putting a fire-resistant roof on your home,

4. putting fire-resistant undersides on decks and balconies,

5. removing dead branches from your roof,

6. making sure your home is easily identifiable from main road,

7. making sure all trees are planted away from structures,

8. making sure all trees are planted away from utility lines,

9. working with neighbors to prune and clear common areas,

10. stacking firewood away from structures, and

11. contacting the local fire department for a personal fire safety inspection.

The options for each item were: 1 = already done, 2 = will do in next month, 3 = will do in next 2–3 months, 4 = will do next year, 5 = probably will not do (0 = not applicable).

The southern Arizona respondents had undertaken significantly fewer defensible space actions. In fact, southern Arizona residents were in sharp contrast to the other three sites when it came to 7 of the 11 risk mitigating actions. Southern Arizona and southern New Mexico respondents

were significantly less likely to undertake the defensible space action of "working with neighbors to clear common areas." In addition, a significant number of respondents from the southern regions stated that they would not undertake this action, unlike respondents from the northern regions of both New Mexico and Arizona. We found that a number of residents in both southern Arizona and northern New Mexico would not undertake the "stacking wood away from structures" action (20% and 25%, respectively), while respondents in southern Arizona were significantly more likely to have undertaken this action (45.5%). We also found that southern New Mexico was the only site where a significant percent of respondents stated that they would not "plant trees away from utility lines" (55%). Finally, for the defensible space action of "contacting the local fire department for a personal fire safety inspection," we found that there was much variation across locations. About 25% of respondents in southern Arizona and both sites in New Mexico had already undertaken this action, while about 25% said they would not do it. In contrast, 50% of respondents in northern Arizona had already undertaken the action, while 30% said they would not take the action. There was variation among the four regions in 7 of the 11 defensible space actions, but there was a pattern among the regions in the other 4 actions (table 4)

If residents believe that certain factors will be effective at mitigating wildfire risks, it seems logical that they will undertake those actions (table 5). We asked residents to tell us how effective they thought each of the risk reduction actions was at preventing wildfires from impacting their property and their lives. The pattern of perceived effectiveness of each of the defensible space actions was consistent across all 4 regions for all 11 actions. For the most part, respondents said they felt that the actions were effective at reducing the risk of wildfires damaging property or injuring individuals—the overall rating was quite high (6.0 out of 7, table 5).

Residents were asked how confident they were in their ability to undertake the 11 risk reduction behaviors (table 6). But it is also important to understand what affects that decision. Implementing these tasks can be very costly both physically and financially. Therefore, we measured respondents' confidence levels at undertaking each of the defensible actions as well as their overall confidence in their ability to protect themselves and their property. A pattern emerged for the degree of confidence (moderately high) that respondents in all locations had in their ability to undertake all but three of the defensible actions. The first was putting fire-resistant undersides to decks and balconies on a home. This lower confidence could have been because some residents did not have balconies and decks, so this was not perceived as relevant to their situation. The second action was planting trees away from houses and structures. The reasoning for this lower confidence level could have been that many people were not willing to cut down trees close to their structures or do not intend to plant more trees. The third action was working with neighbors to clear common areas. This could have been due to the lack of organized HOAs or other community organizations or the desire for isolation from neighbors.

---

[3] These 11 items are based upon information provided by the Fire Safe Council of California.

Table 4. Defensible space actions.

Defensible space action	Overall mean	Arizona		New Mexico	
		northern region	southern region	northern region	southern region
30-foot defensible space	58% already done	64% done already	47.2% already done	65.3% already done	50% already done
Plant fire-resistant plants	56% already done	61.8% already done	38.2% already done	53.5% already done	72.5% already done
Fire resistant roof	62% already done	66.3% already done	47.3% already done	73.5% already done	50% already done
Fire resistant undersides	55% will not do	64.1% will not do	35.2% will not do	45.3% will not do	79% will not do
Remove dead branches	81% already done	77.2% already done	67.3% already done	92.3% already done	90% already done
Easily identify house	83% already done	93.3% already done	63.6% already done	83.8% already done	85% already done
Trees planted away from house	62% already done	66% already done	52.7% already done	63.4% already done	60% already done
Trees planted away from utility lines	63% already done	72.8% already done	52.7% already done	71.8% already done	55% will not do
Work with neighbors	48% already done	57.6% already done	42% already done and 33% will	49.3% already done	55.3% will not do 34.2% already done
Stack firewood away from house	63% already done	68% already done	45.5% already done & 20% will not do	62.8% already done & 25% will not do	68.5% already done
Fire safety inspection	34% already done & 32% will not do	48.9% already done & 37% will not do	21.8% already done & 21.8% will not do	28% already done, 21% do in next 3-6 months, & 24% will not do	30% already done & 45% will not do
Sample size	502	152	119	141	90

Table 5. Effectiveness of each risk reduction action.

Defensible space action	Overall mean (SD)	Arizona		New Mexico	
		northern region	southern region	northern region	southern region
30-foot defensible space	5.31 (2.03)	5.32 (2.06)	5.28 (2.14)	5.37 (1.87)	5.16 (2.23)
Plant fire-resistant plants	5.20 (1.76)	5.36 (1.82)	5.21 (1.41)	4.97 (1.75)	5.26 (2.02)
Fire resistant roof	5.93 (1.54)	6.10 (1.59)	6.17 (0.99)	5.88 (1.56)	5.65 (1.89)
Fire resistant undersides	5.12 (2.04)	5.01 (2.16)	5.55 (1.67)	5.19 (1.86)	4.81 (2.44)
Remove dead branches	6.15 (1.40)	5.94 (1.56)	6.33 (1.28)	6.24 (1.37)	6.24 (1.14)
Easily identify house	5.94 (1.38)	5.97 (1.41)	5.95 (1.10)	5.89 (1.53)	6.00 (1.31)
Trees planted away from house	5.41 (1.81)	5.32 (1.88)	5.38 (1.77)	5.53 (1.66)	5.39 (2.04)
Trees planted away from utility lines	5.28 (1.97)	4.97 (2.07)	5.69 (1.73)	5.49 (1.89)	5.13 (2.35)
Work with neighbors	5.10 (2.12)	4.82 (2.07)	5.47 (2.06)	5.23 (1.89)	5.11 (2.37)
Stack firewood away from house	5.97 (1.69)	5.74 (1.97)	6.21 (1.34)	6.14 (1.42)	5.89 (1.81)
Fire safety inspection	5.23 (1.79)	5.41 (1.83)	5.28 (1.56)	4.90 (1.84)	5.42 (1.83)
Overall effectiveness	6.00 (1.28)	5.96 (1.37)	6.12 (1.15)	5.92 (1.29)	6.02 (1.25)
Sample size	502	152	119	141	90

1 = not at all effective to 7 = very effective

Table 6. Confidence to undertake these defensible actions.

Defensible space action	Overall mean (SD)	Arizona		New Mexico	
		northern region	southern region	northern region	southern region
30-foot defensible space	5.17 (2.35)	5.62 (2.16)	4.58 (2.15)	5.30 (2.15)	4.47 (2.65)
Plant fire-resistant plants	5.71 (1.79)	5.88 (1.74)	5.61 (1.98)	5.62 (1.72)	5.63 (1.86)
Fire resistant roof	5.79 (1.92)	6.20 (1.46)	5.25 (2.30)	5.87 (1.97)	5.26 (2.10)
Fire resistant undersides	4.75 (2.48)	5.31 (2.27)	4.75 (2.57)	4.59 (2.46)	3.73 (2.60)
Remove dead branches	6.30 (1.31)	6.54 (0.92)	5.95 (1.86)	6.27 (1.42)	6.20 (0.94)
Easily identify house	6.35 (1.29)	6.53 (0.97)	5.90 (1.93)	6.58 (0.95)	5.94 (1.45)
Trees planted away from house	4.98 (2.33)	5.13 (2.23)	4.90 (2.41)	5.10 (2.30)	4.54 (2.52)
Trees planted away from utility lines	5.17 (2.47)	5.35 (2.35)	5.32 (2.53)	5.35 (2.37)	4.08 (2.71)
Work with neighbors	4.82 (2.32)	5.07 (2.03)	4.91 (2.44)	4.75 (2.39)	4.21 (2.60)
Stack firewood away from house	6.05 (1.79)	6.13 (1.77)	5.98 (1.93)	6.26 (1.42)	5.47 (2.17)
Fire safety inspection	5.72 (1.72)	5.83 (1.64)	5.60 (2.04)	5.72 (1.69)	5.59 (1.55)
Overall confidence	5.72 (1.20)	5.78 (1.22)	5.98 (1.32)	5.56 (1.04)	5.54 (1.26)
Sample size	502	152	119	141	90

1 = not at all confident to 7 = very confident

4.0 Responsibility

A heightened awareness of risk often translates into a strong sense of individual responsibility among residents for mitigating their risk from future fires. As a fourth generation resident on the Kaibab NF stated, "The majority of people here feel like that is their land, and their responsibility [is] to manage it, take care of it." This perception often resulted in a strong motivation to engage in active treatment and maintenance of one's property. Even with treatment, however, residents understand that they are not immune to the risk of catastrophic fires. As one resident on the Lincoln NF put it, "I don't think anybody, including us, [is] fooled into thinking that we've completely protected ourselves from the wildfire…if anything…we've done enough work that we will have slowed the progress of a ground fire, or even a crown fire…to the point where we could, hopefully, evacuate the site in time and have no human injuries if there were a fire." In fact, it was because of this heightened awareness of the wildfire risk that some reported feeling a low sense of confidence that the treatments they have already done on their property are enough—instead they were wanting "to go back and…clear another deeper layer."

Throughout Region 3, respondents tended to express the opinion that the responsibility for mitigating the risk of catastrophic fire lays with each individual rather than a specific agency. Respondents were nearly three times more likely to express that individuals should be responsible for their own protection than they were to say that the responsibility lays with the FS, and very few respondents think that

responsibility should be shared between the individual and the FS.

Another important factor in understanding the general public's perception of wildfire risks mitigation is to understand where the public places responsibilities for this mitigation process (table 7). The responsibility for protecting oneself, property, and lands is another issue that has been found to determine what homeowners will do to mitigate wildfire risks. We asked the public the degree of responsibility of individual homeowners, HOAs, local governments, and the FS in mitigating the risks of wildfires. The responses continue to help us construct a picture of how residents in the WUI view the process of mitigating wildfire risks for all parties concerned. The results indicate that across all locations, respondents believe strongly that homeowners are responsible for protecting themselves and their property. Likewise, they said they believe that HOAs should be held responsible for protecting homeowners and private property. This could be due to the issue that occurs when some homeowners do little or nothing to mitigate fire risks on their property, resulting in a potentially negative spillover effect on others in the community. Respondents also said they believe that county and city governments along with the public land managers are responsible for working to mitigate wildfire risks. All in all, the overarching belief is that mitigating wildfire risks is the responsibility of all members of the community, including the FS.

Table 7. Responsibility for protecting against wildfires.

Responsibility	Overall mean (SD)	Arizona		New Mexico	
		northern region	southern region	northern region	southern region
Homeowners' responsibility	6.36 (0.94)	6.35 (0.98)	6.43 (0.93)	6.40 (0.88)	6.24 (1.01)
HOA's responsibility	5.83 (1.43)	5.75 (1.45)	6.09 (1.30)	5.67 (1.63)	5.89 (1.21)
Local government responsibility	5.59 (1.52)	5.57 (1.39)	5.62 (1.54)	5.65 (1.55)	5.50 (1.70)
US Forest Service responsibility	5.27 (1.56)	5.11 (1.55)	5.31 (1.59)	5.37 (1.56)	5.31 (1.60)
Sample size	502	152	119	141	90

1 = not at all responsible to 7 = very responsible

5.0 Treatment Options

The threat that wildfire poses to property and lives under current conditions is particularly critical, especially in the WUI, where, as one resident near the Lincoln NF stated, "You can't react fast enough to defend the town...the fires just move too fast when they get going." Therefore, there is a strong belief that the risk of catastrophic fires must be mitigated through human intervention (use of treatments). The presence of differing opinions from stakeholders and interest groups alike, as well as the need to integrate science into the process, presents a challenge to policymakers at the national level and to those who implement the policy locally. Here, we discuss the perceptions of how treatments can best be used to serve the needs of stakeholders and to facilitate the management of public lands to preserve these Forests as national treasures. We discuss prescribed fire, thinning, chemical treatments, and the combination of treatments.

In the survey of the general public, respondents were asked to rate their level of agreement with two statements: "Forest treatment options to reduce the risks of wildfire should be focused around communities/should be implemented across the entire NF" (table 8). Respondents expressed the preference that forest treatment implementation should focus on the entire NF, including wilderness areas, as well as areas around communities using these treatments. Respondents rated a high level of agreement with the statement "Prescribed fires should only be used once the usable wood material is removed through commercial logging/removed through thinning projects."

5.1 Overall Goals and Benefits of Treatment

A group of USFS Region 3 personnel respondents made the point that "what's good for people is not necessarily good for the landscape...." Populations in the WUI are projected to continue increasing, with more and more homes being built in fire-prone areas such as hill slopes where there is a high danger of mudslides, etc. People are also moving into areas prone to stand-replacing fires, thereby increasing the risk of devastating destruction. The Region 3 personnel respondents said they believe that thinning is favored by the public as a treatment option although most thinning projects do not cover the entire landscape. They also said they believe that the public is not being educated about the overall goals, benefits, and risks of each treatment.

While some perceived benefits are unique to a specific treatment, overall the perceived goals and benefits of each treatment are similar: (1) to preserve the ecosystem, (2) to restore forest health, and (3) to mitigate the risk of catastrophic fires. This is represented by the sentiments of a member of the Firewise community adjacent to the Santa Fe NF who stated that to restore "forests so that they can sustain fire without threatening the [health of the] forests or the home" should be the goal. To have a healthy forest requires maintenance. As one resident of the Lincoln NF stated, you cannot just let nature take its course because "[the forests] will continue to burn until [they] all burn down or we thin [them]."

Treatment is seen as vital to reducing the number of trees in the forest, many of which are dead or dying due to beetle infestation. As a representative of the Board of Supervisors in Globe, Arizona, stated, "Our biggest concern now is these dead trees. We need to remove them from the forest so that fuel loadings are reduced. Some of the dead or downed trees are still usable, but if we just let them rot, then it is just more fuel for fires." Reducing density also benefits the forest by decreasing the competition for moisture. This improves the health of the remaining trees, especially in drought

Table 8. Forest treatment options.

Forest treatment preferences	Overall mean (SD)	Arizona		New Mexico	
		northern region	southern region	northern region	southern region
Focus on communities	5.22 (1.52)	5.28 (1.52)	5.10 (1.56)	5.33 (1.48)	5.12 (1.55)
Focus across entire Forest landscape	4.97 (1.85)	4.59 (1.94)	5.39 (1.81)	5.23 (1.66)	4.69 (1.92)
Use fire after commercial logging	4.63 (2.05)	4.46 (1.99)	5.39 (1.81)	5.23 (1.66)	4.69 (1.92)
Use fire after thinning projects	5.22 (1.66)	5.09 (1.60)	5.26 (1.76)	5.50 (1.55)	4.92 (1.77)
Let it burn unless lives are threatened	4.13 (1.91)	4.24 (1.69)	3.78 (2.04)	4.16 (1.94)	4.36 (2.00)
No prescribed fire if smoke is health problem	3.18 (1.74)	3.16 (1.71)	3.07 (1.71)	3.23 (1.78)	3.31 (1.84)
Sample size	502	152	119	141	90

1 = strongly disagree to 7 = strongly agree

Table 9. Effectiveness of various forest management practices.

Effectiveness	Overall mean (SD)	Arizona		New Mexico	
		northern region	southern region	northern region	southern region
Current management practices	4.08 (1.25)	3.93 (1.30)	4.04 (1.03)	4.25 (1.31)	4.13 (1.35)
Current mechanical removal	3.94 (1.33)	3.89 (1.40)	3.65 (1.25)	4.16 (1.34)	4.06 (1.24)
Current thinning projects	3.87 (1.27)	3.91 (1.25)	3.49 (1.17)	3.96 (1.31)	4.18 (1.30)
Current prescribed fire projects	3.87 (1.34)	3.81 (1.43)	3.81 (1.05)	3.99 (1.34)	3.87 (1.51)
Sample size	502	152	119	141	90

1 = not at all effective to 7 = very effective

conditions. As one resident near the Santa Fe NF stated, "[The forest is] so thick with trees that the trees can't get their nutrients, can't get water." Finally, another perceived benefit of reducing the number of trees is allowing grass and vegetation to grow, which is critical to preventing the growth of seedlings and helping to minimize the risk of crown fires. Left untreated, tree crowding not only jeopardizes the health of the forest through increased beetle infestation, but it also increases the threat of catastrophic fire. Table 9 provides the findings on the perceived effectiveness of the treatment options, as currently implemented.

5.2 Overall Challenges to Treatments

A significant challenge to deciding which treatment options should be used and how they should be implemented on the forest was the variety of opinions of different stakeholder groups. A representative of the communities near the Santa Fe NF stated that when it comes to thinning, "it's sort of an informal debate in the public of what's good for the forest. Some of them believe that you shouldn't cut a tree." With regard to prescribed fire, many share the belief expressed by a resident near the Lincoln NF that "people are concerned because they know that controlled burns can get out of hand. Other people are glad that something's being done to help solve the problem."

The biggest challenge, according to some groups that we interviewed, is what are perceived as extremist views held by some environmentalist[4] and special interest groups. These groups were seen as being against many forms of treatment because of the perceived impact of the treatment on wildlife and the ecosystem. Respondents' perceptions can be attributed to the rise in lawsuits that present significant challenges to mitigating wildfire risks. For example, as one resident near the Lincoln NF observed, "The Southwest Center for Biological Diversity (SCBD) has been suing the Fish and Wildlife Service and the FS to stop their forest thinning because they say it threatens the [spotted] owl." There

was an increased perception among the involved laypeople that the NFs are being managed in the courts.

Respondents also said they believe that inflexible laws and regulations are challenges to treatment implementation. Interviewees said they believe these laws are often set by politicians in Washington, DC, who, according to a large number of Region 3 stakeholders, do not have a good understanding of the conditions of the forests. As one resident of the Lincoln NF and member of the Timberon HOA stated, "People who do not live in the forest don't understand the necessity for clearing." This lack of understanding was perceived as causing a lack of political support to make the necessary resources available to mitigate wildfire risks.

Respondents expressed that the challenge of mitigating the threat of catastrophic fire is "a long-term problem" that is only going to get worse. As such, they see the need for treatment to be ongoing because, as a State Farm representative near the Lincoln NF stated, "By the time you get through, then you've got to turn around and re-treat what you treated before." This opinion applies to both public and private lands.

Analysis of the perceptions of challenges to treatment by interviewee type showed a strong shared belief by local experts, involved lay public and environmentalists/special interest groups that the biggest challenge to treatment is the difference in values of the people who make up the forest communities. Local experts and the involved lay public showed an appreciation for the huge undertaking that treatment implementation represents given the current conditions of the forest, as well as the high cost associated with treatment options. The involved lay public respondents said they felt that ordinances or the lack thereof also were obstacles in their ability to carry out treatments. Local experts saw resistance from various groups to treatment as one of their major challenges.[5]

Different perceptions of challenges were also found at the state and local levels. For the State of Arizona, respondents expressed that environmentalists seemed to pose the biggest challenge to people's ability to carry out treatments. At the individual Forest level, however, the Kaibab

[4] Many individuals that we interviewed would frequently refer to "environmentalist" as an obstruction to various treatment options as discussed here. When asked to define the term, they would generally provide examples such as the Southwest Center for Biodiversity, Forest Guardians, and other organizations.

[5] Focus group interviews were used to supplement the results to the open-ended questions in the general survey.

NF managers' biggest challenge seemed to be resistance to treatment; whereas on the Tonto NF, the biggest challenges were ordinances and limited resources for treatment. In New Mexico, the overwhelmingly biggest challenge was the different values and cultures in the population, with the huge undertaking and cost of the various treatments also being important considerations. Another significant concern in the Santa Fe NF was the limited road access that presented problems for wildfire mitigation efforts.

5.3 What Facilitates Treatment

An increased awareness of the conditions on the forests, and the benefits of treatment to mitigate the risk of catastrophic fires that are associated with those conditions, is essential to facilitate treatment. As one resident of the Lincoln NF observed, "People here are aware of the fire danger; and they want something done. And they appreciate when things do get done." Being able to see first-hand the effect of treatment increases the awareness of the benefits of treatment and the willingness to treat. As one HOA representative on the Tonto NF stated, when residents "can see where treatments have occurred and their effect on how fire spread, and you have that evidence…if the house is really cleaned up within the community, it typically didn't burn down. [The fire] basically jumped away from it."

Another factor that facilitates treatment is collaboration among the FS, the local community, and local agencies such as the fire department. As a county representative near the Tonto NF stated, "Any time we can get cooperation, the understanding, we like to have that because enforcement is always the last tool we choose to use, but I think we still have to have it available to us." In addition to having laws and regulations in place, having adequate funding is also critical to facilitating treatment.

Interviewee responses also showed a strong and shared belief by the lay public, local experts, and local government representatives that having the right ordinances in place plays a significant role in facilitating treatments and ensuring that they are effectively undertaken.

5.4 Prescribed Fire

The biggest perceived benefit of prescribed fire was that it is the best way to safely reintroduce fire into the forest after years of suppression. As a resident near the Santa Fe NF stated, "A low to moderate-intensity under-burn would reduce the accumulation of small trees that have sprouted since the last burning. If left unchecked, the small trees and shrubs would develop into fuels, which would contribute to crown fire." This treatment option was the preferred treatment of environmentalists because it is perceived to most closely mimic the natural fire conditions. As a representative from the Arizona Game and Fish Department on the Kaibab NF observed, "The mosaic [prescribed fire] creates—it misses spots and leaves spots and encourages brushy growth, which is important for a lot of wildlife species from a lot of

perspectives." In terms of cost and labor intensity, managed burns are seen as highly effective in treating large areas and especially areas that are difficult to reach.

Perhaps the biggest challenge to carrying out prescribed fire was the fact that conditions need to be "near perfect" before a fire can be ignited. As a member of the Firewise communities near Santa Fe, New Mexico stated, the FS "cannot go and have a controlled burn in the forest…when they've got communities that can potentially be overrun by a fire and destroyed." The right conditions include appropriate weather and adequate fuel loadings and staff to support the treatment. As one Ranger District representative on the Santa Fe NF stated, "making sure nobody [is] off-district, fighting somewhere else" must be a priority determination. Scarce resources present a challenge for carrying out prescribed fire. Because of the limited resources available for fighting fires nationwide, the support needed to carry out prescribed fires is sometimes not available because staff members are being used elsewhere.

Controlling a prescribed fire presents another challenge. There is significant awareness that a burn can easily get out of control and cause devastating effects. This is in no small measure attributed to the fact that, as one resident near the Lincoln NF stated, "…we hear about the ones that get out of control. The ones that weren't, we don't hear about it." Many recognize the benefits of prescribed fire but adopt a "Not in my backyard" attitude out of fear that the FS will lose control of the burn.

Smoke, which is an inevitable part of prescribed fire, is also a challenge. While some are bothered by smoke that is a result of prescribed fire, there is also a significant understanding that is echoed by a resident near the Lincoln NF who stated, "There are some unpleasant aspects of [prescribed fire], but you have to live with it because the benefit is really worth it." Others, however, experience significant health issues as a result of the smoke. To mitigate these issues often means more expense because people have to be given the option and funding to temporarily relocate. The program in Flagstaff, Arizona, that provides the at-risk public with funding to relocate during a prescribed burn is a good example of a proactive policy.

No significant differences could be found when the benefits associated with prescribed fire were analyzed by interviewee type, by forest or by state. Some differences were found, however, in the perception of challenges associated with prescribed fire. At the interviewee type level, local experts and the involved lay public shared a strong belief that smoke presented the biggest challenge to carrying out managed fires. In fact, local experts said the presence of smoke was overwhelmingly the number one challenge to carrying out prescribed fire. Similarly, these groups also shared the strong belief that both the need for conditions to be right before carrying out a prescribed fire and objections from environmentalists and special interest groups constituted the biggest challenges to burning projects.

At the individual Forest and state levels, a strong belief emerged on the Kaibab NF that smoke and health concerns

Table 10. Effectiveness ratings of forest treatment options.

Forest treatment options preferences	Overall mean (SD)	Arizona		New Mexico	
		northern region	southern region	northern region	southern region
Prescribed fire	4.86 (1.50)	4.81 (1.55)	5.11 (1.19)	4.66 (1.51)	4.90 (1.70)
Managing natural ignited fire	4.34 (1.47)	4.42 (1.44)	4.38 (1.46)	4.20 (1.52)	4.37 (1.52)
Selective thinning— (small wood)	5.11 (1.42)	4.85 (1.56)	5.02 (1.34)	5.30 (1.37)	5.33 (1.33)
Selective thinning— (large wood)	4.21 (1.73)	4.07 (1.71)	4.31 (1.68)	4.30 (1.75)	4.21 (1.86)
Prescribed fire and thinning small wood	5.18 (1.44)	5.09 (1.54)	5.46 (1.22)	5.15 (1.44)	5.03 (1.52)
Prescribed fire and logging	4.43 (1.74)	4.38 (1.73)	4.75 (1.76)	4.43 (1.63)	4.10 (1.85)
Goats	4.75 (1.69)	4.63 (1.55)	4.49 (1.81)	5.01 (1.67)	4.92 (1.79)
Salvage logging	4.69 (1.78)	4.50 (1.92)	4.67 (1,69)	4.74 (1.74)	4.96 (1.74)
Thin diseased trees	5.55 (1.54)	5.52 (1.64)	5.54 (1.22)	5.61 (1.51)	5.58 (1.48)
Do nothing	2.08 (1.45)	2.41 (1.69)	1.81 (1.24)	1.83 (1.05)	2.32 (1.66)
Sample size	502	152	119	141	90

1 = not at all effective to 7 = very effective

that were largely associated with smoke were the main challenge to the prescribed fire treatment. Similarly, the presence of smoke was the largest challenge associated with prescribed fire in Arizona. In New Mexico, however, the need for conditions to be right before carrying out a prescribed burn was the number one challenge to prescribed burning, with respondents near the Santa Fe NF being much more likely to see this as a problem.

The results from the survey of the general population provide some support for the belief that prescribed fires are a valued part of forest treatment options (table 10). In the survey, respondents were also asked to rate the effectiveness of managing naturally ignited fires. There were no significant differences across the four regions—the overall sentiment was that this strategy is a moderately effective way to manage public lands for potential fires. However, this sentiment was significantly higher in the southern Arizona area (M = 5.11). This could be due to the region's vegetation type as well as its smaller number of catastrophic fires. According to a local FMO, in many of these areas in southern Arizona, ranchers value prescribed fire as a means of regenerating grasses and removing encroaching woody vegetation.

5.5 Thinning

Thinning was viewed by respondents as the best way to remove fuel from the forest given current conditions that limit the ability to conduct prescribed fire, especially in the WUI. As one homeowner on the Lincoln NF stated, communities are "surrounded by forests…[it is perceived that being] thinned appropriately…would at least give this community a chance if there is a greater fire in the forest." Also, people see utilization of wood as important. They would prefer to see timber utilized for firewood or other uses rather than just burning the potentially valuable natural resource.

Specific challenges associated with thinning small-diameter timber on both public and private lands had to do with concern that too many trees would be taken or that large trees would be logged. There was also a great deal of concern over the removal of big trees, which are seen as the most valuable resource of the forest—"Everybody always wants to know how many and how big." Environmentalists are especially averse to thinning as a treatment option because of what some respondents perceive as their "fear that we're [FS] going to use the sheltered fuel breaks as a timber sale, and we're going to cut larger trees than they want us to cut."

The high-density condition of the forest makes thinning costly and labor-intensive. As one resident near the Santa Fe NF stated, "The cost of taking down trees is enormous." Commercial operations such as mills, logging, and timber industries have in the past been able to take on the cost of removing small-diameter trees because of the value of big trees. Today, most mills and logging companies have left the forests, which presents a problem for these communities with the loss of both jobs and important tax revenues. Because of a renewed interest in utilization, thinning is seen as having potential for stimulating economic development in the forest. However, utilization would be based on small-diameter timber. This constraint raises question over the commercial value of small-diameter products, and further, as one resident near the Santa Fe NF stated,

"Logging companies are not going to go into NFs until there is money to be made." Diameter restrictions pose a challenge because commercial operations to remove small-diameter timber are not profitable due to the high cost of treatment and the lack of a market for the timber. Adding to the cost of large-scale/commercial thinning is the fact that virtually no mills remain in the region, making it necessary to transport logs out of the area. As one timber representative on the Kaibab NF stated, "...transportation in today's logging costs...is about half your cost. You can cut trees and split them and load [them onto a] truck for the same cost, on average, of what it takes to haul them to the mill."

Finally, another concern with thinning is the residual materials such as slash and chipping debris that are the result of these treatments. As one representative of forest management operations on the Lincoln NF stated, "If you put it back in the forest, you still have a fire problem." However, some people said they feel that, despite this challenge, thinning does help because not all fuels are equally volatile. As one timber representative from the Kaibab NF stated, "A ton of fuel falling naturally off the trees—your dead limbs and needles and whatnot—I think is a lot more volatile than this ton of fuel generated from timber harvest activities."

An analysis by interviewee type of the challenges associated with thinning showed that a major challenge to thinning as a treatment option is the fear that thinning will result in "clear cutting" and that the residual material from thinning will lead to more fuel in the forest if not disposed of properly. This is a primary concern for respondents from New Mexico.

When we looked at the results from the survey of the general public in Region 3, we found that selective thinning of small-diameter trees was viewed as moderately effective, while selective thinning of large trees was perceived as less effective. This is similar to the belief voiced by the interviewees in focus groups and in in-depth interviews.

5.6 Chemical Treatments

Chemical treatments are seen as a way of treating the bark beetle infestation without having to remove trees. However, there were many concerns about chemical use and whether it poses exposure risks to community residents. Overall, while there was not a clear understanding of chemical treatment, the perception was that "it's toxic, really toxic;" and chemical treatments were seen as not only harmful to humans but to wildlife as well. This perception was coupled with the fact that when "spraying for noxious weeds, they [FS] were not really informing people of where they were spraying, which is a problem for people who are chemical sensitive." Aerial spraying of chemicals can pose just as much of a challenge because of the inability to control where the chemicals go. Safety issues aside, spraying is viewed as one of the most expensive treatment options at an estimated cost of $2000 per acre.

5.7 Combination of Treatments

There is some belief that the best way to manage the forest is through a combination of treatments. Often, this combination includes thinning and burning. As a resident of the Kaibab NF with an advanced degree in Forestry stated, "Doing both always has the best kick. You only get partial benefit from just burning or thinning." The combination of thinning and burning was viewed by many as "the only way to prevent any major damage from fires getting out of control—to get back to the natural fire regime is to thin it enough and then to burn it."

Due to current forest conditions, thinning is perceived by the public as a necessary first step to remove some of the small growth trees that can easily result in a devastating fire, even with prescribed fire. Similarly, fire is the essential follow up to a thinning treatment because of the residual material that often is left after thinning. As one resident near the Santa Fe NF observed, residents want "to thin and burn the slash because you wouldn't gain anything by cutting down all the trees and brush and leaving the slash there." Slash or chips that are left after thinning need to be removed so that they do not create additional ground fuel. Burning is the most labor- and cost-effective way of dealing with this residual material. As one District Ranger representative on the Santa Fe NF stated, "If we can get in there and do mechanical treatment and use prescribed fire, we can maintain an ecosystem that's at low risk to the type of catastrophic fires that are threatening homes and watersheds and everything else."

In the survey of the general public, respondents said they believe that a combination of prescribed fire and thinning (preferably small wood rather than large trees) is a moderately effective strategy. Similar to the results from the comparison of the two types of thinning treatments (small versus large), prescribed fire with small timber thinning was preferred significantly more than with large trees (table 10).

5.8 Characteristics of Successful Treatment Projects

Characteristics of some of the most successful treatment projects include a high level of awareness of the need for and benefit of treatment, and available funding and good cooperation among neighbors and between the community and the FS. Successful programs are often those where, as one retired Fire Chief on the Tonto NF stated, people are "[encouraged]...to clean up their properties, both from a risk reduction and forest health standpoint. And, if they do that, then we give them a place where they can get rid of materials for free rather than having to pay a fee at the local landfill." Consistent with the qualitative interviews, the "do nothing" strategy was not perceived as a viable alternative for any of the regions.

In the survey of the general public, respondents were asked to rank their top three preferred treatment options,

Table 11. Preferred treatment options.

Treatment option	All locations	Arizona		New Mexico	
		northern region	southern region	northern region	southern region
Most preferred treatment option	Selectively thinning small-diameter trees	Selectively thinning small-diameter trees	Selectively thinning small-diameter trees and diseased trees (salvage logging)	Selectively thinning small-diameter trees	Selectively thinning small-diameter trees
Second most preferred treatment option	Salvage logging and using goats	Thinning and logging diseased trees	Salvage logging	Goats to reduce brush and vegetation	Goats to reduce brush and vegetation
Third most preferred treatment option	Thinning and logging diseased trees	Salvage logging	Thinning and logging diseased trees	Thinning and logging diseased trees	Thinning and logging diseased trees

and, for the most part, the results were remarkably consistent across all four regions (table 11). What emerged from this analysis is that overall, respondents prefer treatment options that do not involve the use of prescribed fire although they recognize the effectiveness of this treatment (tables 10 and 11). Selective thinning, salvage logging, and thinning diseased/infested trees were consistently preferred by respondents. The one exception was that the use of goats as a means to reduce brush and vegetation was preferred in New Mexico. Another interesting point that emerged is that selectively logging large-diameter trees was not preferred by respondents in any region along with the option of doing nothing. It should be noted that these preferences were ranked without considering the cost to implement the various treatment options.

Additionally, other types of treatments that were not discussed in the qualitative (interviews) study but that were measured in the quantitative (mail) survey included the possibility of using goats to reduce fuel loadings, salvage logging from trees that were blown down or burnt, and thinning diseased trees from bark beetle infestations. These strategies were viewed as effective across all of the regions, but there was a significant difference between perceived effectiveness ratings for the three treatments. Thinning diseased trees was viewed significantly higher than using goats or salvage logging (M = 5.55 versus 4.75 and 4.69, respectively; table 10). Overall, the results showed that "doing nothing to mitigate wildfire risks" was not perceived as a desirable option by the public. This is also seen when looking at the means by location. What is interesting is that, for the most part, there was a consistent perception of effectiveness of each of the treatment options across all four sites.

5.9 Trends Within Each Region

Another way to look at the preferences that the general public had for the various types of forest treatment options is by each region (table 11). A description of the ordering of these preferences provides an overview by region that can be partially explained by each region's ecosystem characteristics, fire history, and socio-cultural and economic attributes.

The northern Arizona respondents had strong preferences for (1) thinning diseased trees, (2) using prescribed fires combined with thinning of small-diameter trees, (3) thinning of small-diameter trees, (4) using prescribed fires, and (5) using goats as a way to thin fire-prone underbrush. There were small variations in preferences for the southern region of Arizona: (1) thinning diseased trees, (2) using prescribed fires combined with thinning of small-diameter trees, (3) using prescribed fire, (4) thinning of small-diameter trees, and (5) using prescribed fire combined with large-diameter logging. The difference that stands out most between the two regions is the preference for using goats compared to the preference for using prescribed fire combined with large-diameter logging.

The two New Mexico regions were very similar in their preference ordering for treatment options with only a minor difference in salvage logging and the use of goats. Northern New Mexico respondents had stronger preferences for (1) thinning diseased trees, (2) thinning of small-diameter trees, (3) using prescribed fire combined with thinning of small-diameter trees, (4) using goats as a means to thin fire-prone underbrush, and (5) salvage logging. The southern New Mexico region had a preference ordering of (1) thinning diseased trees, (2) thinning of small-diameter trees, (3) using prescribed fire combined with thinning of small-diameter trees, (4) salvage logging, and (5) using goats as a means to thin fire-prone underbrush.

5.10 The Role of the Forest Service

"The role of the FS is to focus on our lands…play a big role in emergency response…but we can't be an all-encompassing fire service," said a Region 3 management team member. The FS works in close cooperation with the state since the state represents the non-Federal lands, but problems arise when the public thinks that the FS will put all fires out. The agency is now moving away from "putting out the fire by 10 a.m. which encourages the mentality of suppress all wildfires…."

Overall, there appeared to be a general dissatisfaction with the role that the FS has played in managing the forests. Poor management by the FS is seen by respondents as the primary reason for the conditions that have created the threat of catastrophic fires. As one homeowner on the Lincoln NF stated, "It has all started with the fact that [the FS is] not thinning the forest. We've got wildfire problems, we've got drought problems, and we've got fire problems, all because the forest is not getting thinned." Frustration sets in further with the belief that "most of the people in the FS that have the responsibility for management, they know what needs to be done" but they fail to take action. The FS has been seen as trying to manage around the needs of all stakeholders, but there is disagreement so a consistent policy isn't followed. As one fifth-generation resident of the Lincoln NF stated, "I think the way about it is for the District Rangers to make some management decisions…and do their job, and they're not doing that."

In the general population survey, respondents were asked to rate how effective the FS is at managing public lands to reduce the risk of fire, implementing commercial logging programs, implementing thinning projects, and implementing prescribed fire programs on NF lands (see Appendix C: table 4).

In general, respondents had a neutral evaluation of the effectiveness of these policies. This could be due to respondent's lack of knowledge about the effectiveness of FS management policies or how to determine their effectiveness.

Despite a significant level of dissatisfaction voiced by the involved lay public with regard to management by the FS, there is a great deal of public understanding of the constraints the FS faces in trying to carry out its responsibilities. Not the least of these constraints is the nature of the FS as a "national [bureaucracy]," and as one resident of the Lincoln NF stated, it is "run on the political opinion of the whole nation." The agency depends on congressional support for funding and is held to regulations, such as National Environmental Policy Act (NEPA), that are seen as inflexible to guide its management policy, which limits the ability of rangers to make decisions based on local or changing conditions. This is viewed as a significant challenge since there is a general belief that, as one timber representative on the Kaibab NF stated, the FS has skilled and knowledgeable "personnel [who] know how to manage the resource, they know how to get certain results. The problem is regulations tie them in knots."

As one County Representative on the Tonto NF stated, without funding, "the NEPA process and all of the other things that need to be done, [the FS] can't get out in front of anything…[and it is] always reacting." Given current conditions on the forest and the immense job of treating the forest, people said they understand that there is no "possibility of the FS ever having enough money to thin and carry away [enough of] the trees and the brush" to bring it back to a manageable state, stated a resident on the Santa Fe NF.

Lawsuits also create a challenge for the FS in carrying out its duties. According to the Region 3 Fire and Aviation Management Team, "…the agency has had litigation over fire and fuels management, especially over mechanical treatments…." There have been some lawsuits against the fire management plans on the Lincoln, Carson, Apache-Sitgreaves, and the Tonto NFs. Those plans have been withdrawn and fire use has been halted until the problems are resolved.

As one member of the Globe, Arizona, Board of Supervisors stated, "Lawsuits from the environmentalists always put a stop to [treatments]. We try to understand that… and we are trying to cooperate with them." However, doing so is both time consuming and costly and takes away from the agency's efforts on the ground. As one FMO puts it, the agency has "…analysis paralysis. We analyze and we plan and we do all of these things to the best possible ninth degree that you can go to but we don't ever get it implemented and down on the ground and working." As the same FMO put it, the ability of the FS to move projects along at a quicker pace is dependent on "changes in legislation or policy or more authority given out here on the local level for rangers or supervisors."

When looking at how the role of the FS is evaluated by interview type, the involved lay public had strong opinions concerning agency shortcomings. Residents said they view poor communication by the FS as their biggest concern, followed closely by the perception that the FS staff is ineffective, that the FS is unresponsive, and that not enough treatment is being done by the agency. Likewise, strong opinions are present when looking at strengths of the FS. The involved lay public, environmentalists, and local government representatives tended to express that they have a good working relationship with the FS. Residents tended to believe that the FS is doing a good job of communicating with them individually.

At the forest level, strong opinions on the shortcomings of the FS are visible around the Santa Fe NF, where interviewees tended to express the opinion that the FS has ineffective staff and that they are not doing enough treatment of the forests to mitigate the risk of catastrophic fires. Other major concerns for this group are that the FS communicates poorly with the community and that the FS is unresponsive to the needs of the community.

However, some respondents near the Santa Fe NF said they feel very strongly that they have a good working relationship with the FS and also that the FS has a good and knowledgeable staff and that they know action is needed on the forest to mitigate the risk of fire. On the Kaibab NF, respondents not only said they feel like they have a good relationship with the FS but also that the agency does well at communicating with them and that adequate action is being taken by the FS to mitigate the risk of catastrophic wildfire. Finally, respondents from the Lincoln NF also said they feel that they have a good working relationship with the agency, and they feel strongly that the FS actions to mitigate risk are for the benefit of the community.

6.0 Trust in the Forest Service

Trust has been shown to be critical to gain and maintain public acceptance of an institution and its plans, strategies, and management decisions. Research on "social trust" for public agencies such as the FS has found that the amount of trust the public has in the FS has a direct impact on the public's acceptance of fire management policies (e.g., Winter and Cvetkovich 2008). Winter and Cvetkovich (2008) indicate that the social trust in FS policies has dropped recently, not as a result of a loss of confidence but rather that the concerned public "…requires more information than they had in the past to arrive at determinations of trust…." The presence or absence of trust in the FS is strongly related to positive feelings concerning the agency, and it seems to result from both historic and contemporary factors. Agency communication patterns and education efforts also play into the trust equation. Comments from respondents in several geographic locations indicated a lack of trust from the following perceptions of the agency, its personnel, and its programs. More commonly expressed views were the beliefs that the FS is politically driven, is authoritarian and not collaborative, is unresponsive to the concerns of communities, is overly afraid of litigation, and speaks with multiple voices (fire suppression versus ecological perspectives, for example). Concerning litigation, a community activist told us, "I think the FS also overreacts to the threat of lawsuits to the point that they give up on projects simply because the threat is there." In addition, many consider the agency to be highly bureaucratic. As one stated, "They may be technical people, but they're basically bureaucrats. They get tied up in the paperwork and nothing ever gets done."

Trust levels do vary within the geographic areas under study—seemingly related to historic relationships, communication, and agency education/outreach programs, among other factors. In order to examine this variation, we discuss trust levels, communication, and education efforts from the four locations considered in this study.

6.1 Trust Issues—Kaibab NF

Interviews with those associated with the Kaibab NF indicated trust issues derived from regional and national environmental/advocacy groups. One group questioned the credibility of the FS to discuss wildfire risk. As one respondent said, "I think it's important for it to be run by an independent body. I don't think the agency has the credibility to [educate the public about wildfire risk]. That's my opinion." Some said they believe that there is confusion concerning whether the agency wishes to suppress all high-intensity fires or to return fire safely to the ecosystem (as preferred by the group). Additionally, perceived political influences on the forest do not promote trust and credibility. The notion that environmentalists are causing destructive wildfires, presumably promoted by the agency, has been very destructive for environmental groups and their trust in the FS. However, one environmental group member noted that on a recent fire, the Kaibab NF did not take "…cheap shots at anyone. The message was fire is good, they finally moved away from blaming environmentalists to 'look we've suppressed fire for 70 years, we're going to let these things burn.'" Another environmental group said they do not trust the FS on the north rim of the Grand Canyon because the agency is using categorical exclusions in the NEPA process and taking out larger trees in thinning projects. Rhetoric surrounding the Healthy Forest Initiative has also caused mistrust. Respondents from extractive user groups also mentioned a lack of trust on the Kaibab NF that stems from declining timber production in local forests that has negatively affected jobs and community employment.

6.2 Trust Issues—Tonto NF

Interviews conducted in central Arizona near the Tonto NF showed strong trust between local fire professionals and FS fire officials with very positive relations on both sides (feelings that were also heard from stakeholders on the Kaibab NF). Individual working relationships and personal interaction contribute to these good relations. Tonto NF fire personnel stressed that they work hard to maintain good communications and relations with local communities, the County Board of Supervisors, and the Native American populations. One cooperator added the following when discussing local FS officials: "I have no real complaints about cooperation from our local rangers or supervisor. When we get beyond that [with regional or National FS people] is where we don't have as close a relationship on a day-to-day [basis] or as much contact as we'd like to have."

Local government officials were divided in their opinions of the agency. Some county officials said they feel that there is not a joint effort between the county and the Tonto NF in determining priorities and policy direction. For example, the local government works well with the Tonto NF on wildfire issues and burn pits but not on managing the forest. These forest management problems lead to a lack of trust between the county government and the FS. These specific forest management problems deal with grazing and stocking rates on the forest. A County Supervisor told us, "We are not getting the cooperation from the FS that we feel maybe we should have. We should be communicating a little bit more and [be allowed] to participate in those communications [discussions]." The county officials praised the Forest Supervisor and District Rangers for their cooperation on fire issues with the county. They feel they also get cooperation from officials in Washington, DC, but feel frustrated with the amount of time it takes for decisions to filter down through the agency. They also stressed the importance of direct contact with local agency people.

In general, members of the public expressed trust for people they have worked with through the Regional Payson Area Project (RPAP) that includes the FS, and they feel the RPAP people know what they are doing. One interviewee stated, "Most people expect that the FS, if they're given the task of management, they should be managing [the forest] in a responsible way." He also said that often, people do not understand that it takes a long time to implement actions with the laws, costs, and agency structure that are associated with management. According to one Tonto NF employee, most local people seem to support active forest management, while some of the regional environmental groups are opposed and seek litigation opportunities. Opposition from environmental groups to targeted activities is common across the forests of the region. Variation seems to relate to the nature of the forest's resources and its management activity level.

6.3 Trust Issues—Santa Fe NF

Moving into northern New Mexico, we began our interviews with communities, user groups, and the general public near the Santa Fe NF. A large portion of the land in northern New Mexico is former Spanish land grants that were lost by local communities after the U.S. conquest of Mexico in 1848. Much of this land now lies within NF boundaries. Many local people said they believe that the Federal government and the FS took the land away from the Hispanic people of the area and that now the FS is not responsive to their needs. As one land grant member told us, "[The FS is] not that receptive to our concerns. That's a big problem they have. They won't talk to us. They don't talk to us. We write them letters and yet they [don't] talk to us."

A local activist stated that many long-time residents believe that the land was taken care of by their ancestors before it went to the FS—now, it has been clear cut and is overgrown. Many Hispanic residents and ranchers who responded to the interviews said they are frustrated with the FS and its perceived lack of respect for the body of traditional knowledge and experience on the land that is provided by the residents. They feel the FS does not respect traditional forest uses such as ranching, fuel wood gathering, and small logging operations. One person summed up the feeling that "…the FS must understand that these are *our* lands historically." Thus, there is a long tradition of distrust surrounding the Santa Fe NF that manifests itself in many difficulties that FS staff members encounter when working with local communities.

In addition, both logging industry representatives and environmentalists said they distrust the motives and commitments of the FS. Logging industry representatives had the opinion that the FS is not sincere and cannot provide/guarantee a supply of smaller-diameter materials for retooled mills. The environmental groups, many headquartered in Santa Fe, distrust FS thinning projects, believing they are excuses to restart logging programs. As one group member stated, "… [there] is the feeling of distrust that they are going to hide the concept—the idea of logging large trees under the guise of forest restoration."

Many interviewees noted that some District Rangers do not live in the community where they work, creating a rift between the FS and the local community. The agency practice of moving personnel, especially District Rangers, is seen as a significant barrier to continuing communication and developing trust. In addition, many said they are frustrated with agency decisions, which they feel are politically driven and do not favor local communities. In general, interview results indicated that residents near the Santa Fe NF have a higher level of public distrust and negative views concerning communication than any of the other Forests we studied.

6.4 Trust Issues—Lincoln NF

Respondents from the northern section of the Lincoln NF expressed higher trust levels than those surrounding other Forests (significantly more than the Santa Fe NF). Comments such as "the FS are the experts," "the FS knows best," and "the FS has the responsibility to manage the forest and knows what needs to be done" were common. Many user groups, visitors, and local officials indicated productive relationships with the FS, featuring effective communication and collaboration.

On the other hand, some veteran resource users and resource-dependent communities do not share the high level of trust shown by others. Many veteran loggers said they do not trust the agency—they are not willing to be "beaten down" by the FS again, feeling that the FS now awards the few remaining logging and thinning contracts to minorities. Most of the interviewed ranchers said they support the Lincoln NF's burning policies and would like them to be more aggressive. The ranchers indicated a willingness to work with the agency to get the burning done. Many residents throughout the forest suggested that the FS would do more if it could but "their hands are tied" due to the Endangered Species Act and the threat of litigation from environmental groups.

There is concern about working with the Lincoln NF as a partner because of the fear that the FS will not be able to accomplish the work. Most seemed to believe that the agency has good intentions to treat and manage FS lands but is often constrained by planning requirements. This is a somewhat more positive view than was demonstrated on the other Forests (especially on the Santa Fe NF) and by some in the southern section of the Lincoln NF, where various amounts of intentionality are attributed to FS inaction. "[There is]… politics up here [and] the FS is a huge target and they get blamed for everything…. Nobody up here trusts the FS, individuals yes, but…"

There are more problems with trust in the southern portion of the Lincoln NF. This portion of the forest has more threatened and endangered species that must be considered, and the communities are more resource-dependent. A few people in the area voiced the opinion that the Federal government should not own land that it cannot effectively manage. Some said they feel that the FS simply does not have the commitment to complete projects, and this is exemplified with a "we can't do it mentality." "...'paralysis by analysis' is what they've got...it's the culture of their organization [and] the people that are in it have been brought to thinking that 'my hands are tied.'" One Government official said he/she feels that the FS is too concerned with national interests to be responsive to local people.

Treatment projects move along more rapidly in the northern portion of the Lincoln NF (which has fewer threatened and endangered species, more resources, and the proactive community of Ruidoso), and FS approval and trust are stronger in this area. However, some homeowners feel that the agency is not doing enough to take care of its land, which then poses a fire threat to adjacent private land. As was common in all of our interviews, members of the local fire departments throughout the forest are very supportive of the FS, feeling that the Lincoln NF is working closely with them and treating them as partners. Many survey respondents feel that the FS should partner with local governments and communities and stand up to the environmental group threats of litigation in order to accomplish desired projects.

7.0 Communication and Collaboration

Communication and collaboration between the FS, other agencies, user groups, and communities elicits both positive and negative comments concerning the forests of the region. Effective communication is exemplified by the Southwest Region Fire Group that is part of the Southwest Coordinating Group (SWCG). One environmental group leader on the Kaibab NF stated, "I feel that our ability to communicate and collaborate with the FS here is the worst it's ever been." High turnover among FS employees is viewed as a major part of the problem. Lack of continuity in staffing is seen as a problem not only on the Kaibab NF but also on all of the forests in the study area. Both environmental and industry group members expressed that the undesirable mobility of staff results in a loss of institutional and community knowledge. Thus, there is what is viewed as a lack of consistency in how the FS interacts with the public and makes decisions.

Some respondents said it is easier to collaborate with the BLM. Essentially, they indicated that members of the BLM are more willing to collaborate and engage in a transparent way with no screens between the agency and the collaborators. This perception may be related to agency culture. The FS officials seem to feel "[they] are the experts and that's that," according to one environmental group leader. Those who work with the Kaibab NF said the agency has moved back into an authoritarian posture and away from collaboration because collaboration has not provided what the agency wanted. Conflict has not been reduced to the level the agency wanted to get its job done.

Despite trust issues between environmental and user groups on the Kaibab NF, many respondents from HOAs, adjacent communities, and user groups said they believe that personnel of the Kaibab NF communicate relatively well on a variety of issues and levels. Many said they feel that the FS does a good job of notifying people about prescribed fires and wildfires, paying particular attention to those with smoke sensitivities. Others disagreed, stating that the FS could do a better job of notifying people who are sensitive to smoke. As one resident stated, "Smoke is real, it bothers people, and smoke needs to happen. We need to stop pretending it's not going to happen and actually deal with how it's going to happen and educate people and set up programs to help people who have health problems with it when it is happening." Many said they feel that the Flagstaff Fire Department does an excellent job with this task. The city program that pays for people to leave the area during city fires was viewed very favorably. Others feel that the impact of smoke on the tourist sector warrants further consideration. The problem of smoke appears to be a much bigger issue on the Kaibab NF than on the other regional Forests. This may be because of wind conditions in the area. It could also be that smoke problems are just beginning to emerge as a regional issue in the area of the Grand Canyon.

An interviewee stated that the Kaibab NF is responsive to the public and leadership seems to know what it is doing. On the other hand, others complained that the Forest employees are non-responsive, do not return calls, and do not get the word out about burning. This latter point was exemplified in the quote by one interviewee who stated that "…when I have called to complain, it's always I'm the only person on the planet who has ever called and complained, which I know is not true if you talk to other people."

Several interviewees indicated that they have better relations with the Kaibab NF than with other agencies and Forests. A Flagstaff city employee said he/she believes that the city and the Forest staffs communicate well, while another respondent added that the agency is good about asking for comments and soliciting public opinions. "As far as coordination with the FS and communication and relations between the city and the district…I personally and professionally, in my, in my position here, have never had a problem. They have been overly helpful." FS employees also were of the opinion that communication has improved over the years. With some exceptions, relatively good communication between the FS and local governments was noted on all of the Forests studied. Professionals from varying agencies may "speak the same language," leading to positive views regarding communication.

Suggestions for better communication in the area included calls for greater coordination among agencies involved in fire management. Again, some groups blamed poor communication for a high turnover rate of forest employees, while others stressed that they have positive discussions with local employees but that the "true" decision-makers at the FS are "back east" or in Washington, DC. Over and over, the importance of local, personal contact using both formal and informal techniques was mentioned—not only on the Kaibab NF but also on the Tonto, Santa Fe, and Lincoln NFs. It seems that there is much greater trust and communication when people know the local agency personnel, develop relationships with them, and feel comfortable with them.

One concern about communication that was voiced by residents near the Tonto NF is that the FS does not "get out" the need for volunteers and volunteer work. Much volunteer work can be difficult to coordinate and communicate, but the consensus among these interviewees was that the community is willing and able to help out. This type of comment was not heard on any of the other Forests. An increased use of volunteer programs was seen by interviewers as a way to build trust between the FS and the community.

There were complaints from the public affected by the Rodeo-Chediski Fire that people did not receive enough specific information concerning where the fire was burning, the condition of their property, and when they could return home. One FS employee stated that residents "…want to know when they can go home, and, again I just think it was unrealistic, but I'm wondering if there was a way to communicate with them [so] that [they] would have calmed down. Instead of just 'can't give you that' or 'I don't know.'" Gaps in communication relate to the often heard call for closer coordination between fire management agencies. Suggested reasons for communication gaps included mistakes in dispatch and differing perceptions of fire danger and risk between Federal agencies and individual fire chiefs.

Other problems included complaints that the Tonto NF does not follow up on requests (even those from Congressional representatives), presents answers to the public instead of listening to the public, gives opinions on forest condition but never seeks solutions from the public, and does not define terms, such as thinning. On the other hand, many groups stressed ways in which communication is improving. A local fire department employee described activity-defined communications and the importance of identified contacts within the county and at the FS as examples. Information on interviewees' opinions of solid communication sources again stressed the importance of both formal and informal communication channels and direct, local contacts.

The pattern seen on the Kaibab and Tonto NFs concerning positive relations between local and agency professionals also held true on the Santa Fe NF. An official from the city of Santa Fe said he/she feels that "[the FS has] been very cooperative in terms of communicating with us as to what they're currently doing and what they plan to do in the future." Local government officials (both Hispanic and Anglo) expressed much greater trust in the agency and seemed to be much more supportive of its actions and communications than other stakeholders. An example is the communication that exists between the local government and the Forest in notifying government officials of the timing of prescribed fire and related projects.

A major factor in improving communication and trust is solid cooperation between the agency and the public. A number of interviewees in the communities surrounding the Santa Fe NF commented that the Forest representatives only interact with local people when they want something. "Of course, [the FS] did a lot of talking when they had the fire because they needed our cooperation and stuff like that because they had to access the fire from the [land] grant. The fire started in their land and burned into our land." In addition, the agency is viewed as having poor communication skills, as seen in such statements as: "The District Ranger is never available, nor does he return phone calls." "Region 3 has no ability to communicate with communities—they must stand up to the environmentalists and really listen to communities." Several community facilitators said they believe that the FS in Region 3 uses or withholds communication with the public as a means of wielding power and control over the public.

Other respondents on the Santa Fe NF said they feel that communication within the FS is flawed. One facilitator activist stated that there is no mechanism to transfer knowledge from the Research Branch to the National Forest System and vice versa—such as between fire ecologists and fire managers. Others said they feel there is poor communication between varying FS levels—such as districts, the supervisor's office, and the regional office. "Nothing makes its way up or down the hierarchy." "There's lots of moving parts and nothing gets done." This view was also held by county government officials working with the Tonto NF.

A number of stakeholders on the Lincoln NF said they would like to see the FS not just talk about project proposals, but listen to others and work together toward solving some of the long-term problems. They also said they feel that people who have lived in the area for a long time should be recognized by the FS as valuable resources with a considerable amount of knowledge and practical experience. This group expressed that communication should be a two-way process. One state official in the area had the opinion that, historically, the National Forest System side of the FS does not work very well with its communities, but she is seeing pockets of FS activity and improvement within this realm. She said she believes that it helps to have the Regional Forester telling the Forest Supervisors and District Rangers "you will [do this project]." The FS, in her view, should stand up and make decisions since they are "the experts."

Positive comments on communication were also presented by various stakeholders. "We had a conversation and our relationship with the FS, I think, is good. It's very good. I feel very open with communication and up front; of course they have their priorities, and we have ours, but we usually get along well." Members of the small-diameter wood business owners on the Lincoln NF found the FS very helpful in facilitating and maintaining two-way communication between the agencies and the businesses. The Mescalero Tribe would like to see more communication and collaboration with the local ranger district about thinning and burning projects. As mentioned previously, local fire department employees said they believe the FS is visible and available and communicates well with them.

An important aspect of effective public outreach that was noted by many people throughout this area is identifying key members of Federal, State, and local governments and utilizing their interpersonal skills to communicate the important messages. Other respondents said they believe that neighborhood communication and action spurs homeowner motivation, especially among part-time homeowners, where communication can sometimes be difficult.

8.0 Education Programs

The overall response was that the FS needs to take advantage of "teachable moments" right after fires. The FS does a good job of getting information out to the public, although it may not be what they want to hear (Region 3 Fire & Aviation Management Team). "We are giving information but we are not getting feedback from the public. We need to keep in mind that agencies and homeowners have different objectives—the public wants their concerns heard and they want to know what is going on during fires and in preparation for fires." The Kaibab NF is known for its fire education programs, with many positive comments for the Fire Information Officer. The Forest is involved in presentations at local venues and festivals and provides forest tours as well as tours to demonstration properties that show examples of defensible space. "[The FS is] actively involved in trying to disseminate information, and they do a good job of that. They put on tours and get people out there. They are really involved with the Forest Festival." Although we received some comments indicating that the FS could do a better job of educating the public about the benefits of prescribed fire and defensible space, most respondents said they feel the Forest is doing a good job. FS staff is also involved in Kindergarten through 12th grade conservation education efforts, with a specifically tailored program for each grade. A large portion of the program focuses on fire-related issues. "We have a K through 12 program, which we've had for some time. We've actively pursued reverse learning, come in and teach the kids and let them teach the parents. It's quite effective. It's easier for kids to come to it and learn it, often, than it is for older people."

The Tonto NF has partnered with local fire departments, for example RPAP, and has put information on the timing of prescribed fire on the radio and in the newspaper. The Tonto NF outreach efforts include visits by Smokey Bear to schools; distributing flyers, brochures, and homeowner Firewise information; and setting up large displays at public events. A FS interviewee discussed partnership efforts: "We partner a lot with the Globe Fire Department…. They partner with us on a lot of public education during the summer months…. We've actually hired one of their people as a Public Information Officer." The Tonto NF has hired several people to provide full-time public involvement concerning fire prevention information, school presentations, homeowner education programs, and media education programs.

Interviews with staff in the Supervisor's Office in Santa Fe indicated that the staff felt that typical public involvement processes for fire education are not effective. The staff is interested in understanding the local communities' views and attitudes concerning wildfire and prescribed fire. They feel that with a better awareness of their public, they will be able to better educate people and more effectively target education programs. They feel that effective communication is vital to their success and they recognize the importance of interactive, on-the-ground communication. As one staff member said, "Communication is important and the face-to-face—really taking time to discuss those concerns." Unfortunately some staffers stated that the FS does not have enough money for these types of programs, thereby hindering public acceptance of proposed projects. The FS has more requests than it can handle from the public regarding defensible space, requesting help with slash removal, and providing chippers for the communities. The public wants FS communications to be in clear, understandable language—no jargon. Everyone that we interviewed said they believe that the Firewise program is an effective homeowner education and communication tool for the FS in conducting fire risk mitigation efforts. As another staff member said, "The Firewise projects that are going on, I think, has been really good in terms of being a mechanism to communicate with the public and giving us some tools to go and to be able to explain what it is we're doing."

Personnel on the Jemez District of the Santa Fe NF said they believe that long-term residents are more active in wildfire hazard mitigation actions than residents who have recently moved to the area. In their opinion, the Firewise communities have been effective in organizing communities into undertaking risk reduction actions through state implementation grants. The Jemez District has provided support to Firewise efforts by doing individual home hazard analysis, where needed, and by providing information and guidance. The personnel offer "chipper days" and find places where the community can take its residual slash. The FS believes that these communities understand that fuel reduction work needs to happen on both private and Federal properties to be most effective.

Members of the public reiterate some of the concerns of the Supervisor's Office staff on education, while adding others. They also believe that public meetings do not educate effectively; they suggest door-to-door communication as a good way to get communities involved. There is much support for the FS providing education programs on the bigger picture of living with fire in the Southwest, restoring the forest, and discussing the necessity of fire as a part of the ecosystem. As one homeowner put it, "Let people know that this is how it is."

On a positive note, residents of the WUI and Firewise communities rely on the FS for knowledge and community outreach. Most of these people find key individuals in the agency on whom they can rely for accurate information. Several FS people were commended for their outreach abilities. In the Cuba District of the Santa Fe NF, the community is very supportive of the FS in this regard. The Cuba District employees said they believe they are effective at motivating people in this area to undertake defensible space measures on their property. They feel they have a good track record with prescribed fire and that the public trusts them. Still, communication skills are perceived to be lacking on other areas of the Santa Fe NF, and the public recommends that the Forest hire people who know how to communicate with diverse communities.

Almost universally, interviewees support FS education on the benefits of prescribed fire and natural ground fire. These homeowners believe that having the FS or local fire department do a home site visit or property risk assessment is very effective. However, the person who provides the assessment should listen to residents' concerns and not dictate what should be done. A homeowner attested to the effectiveness of the FS inspector by saying, "...he made the same talk 30 times. He was very patient. ...they didn't tell people what they had to remove or anything. Let me make it very clear—very diplomatic." Some residents said they would like to see the FS be flexible and offer options to homeowners concerning mitigation programs. "You can still have trees; creating defensible space does not mean clear cutting." Examples of other mitigation options are increasing insurance rates, stacking firewood away from houses, and cleaning the roof.

As mentioned on the Tonto NF, FS and County Fire Risk Reduction pamphlets should feature pictures of regional or local topography and home styles that seem relevant to the targeted audience. Other outreach suggestions from local facilitators included using local venues such as HOA meetings to get the fire message out; using non-confrontational, science-based approaches (such as the Nature Conservancy's Fire Learning Network); and using neighborhoods and schools. The facilitators advocated a listen and educate approach with positive reinforcement because forcing a fire risk agenda on homeowners does not work. Despite serious trust and communication problems with various groups and communities near the Forest, many of the WUI residents apparently desire FS assistance and are willing to listen to fire risk mitigation messages.

A major topic of communication among the stakeholders on the Lincoln NF was the way in which the agency communicates its fire message and conducts its education programs. Some people said they believe the FS should focus on educating about wildfire risks and what to do to reduce the risks of wildfires. One stakeholder noted, "People who live in or adjacent to the NFs need to realize that it's a risk they take if they live here." There is a fairly pervasive belief in this part of the state that schools and youth should be targeted for wildfire education. One person said they believe that public outreach about "responsible use" of the forest should be paramount and that the FS needs to "find a better way to [communicate with]...the public through a new ad campaign." Other suggestions include working with volunteer groups, such as the boy scouts or girl scouts, making presentations in schools and churches to get parents involved, sending out information in the mail, and utilizing films and documentaries to demonstrate that "thinned" homes are the ones that are often saved in a forest fire. The local fire department is also very active in working with homeowners through Firewise workshops and home inspections and by sending out flyers and listening to concerns.

The FS holds monthly public meetings in the southern part of the Lincoln NF and attends the local fire department meetings, which is viewed by many as effective public outreach. However, one stakeholder said he/she believes that the FS needs to commit time and resources to educate, listen, and make presentations at local clubs—involving the public early and often in decisions regarding forest health and prescribed fire. Further, the FS should undertake a "non-traditional" public involvement process, where decision-makers should listen to the public and "do what someone wants to do from time to time instead of just saying thanks for your input and they are just going through the motions."

The 20 Communities Cost Sharing Program (administered through New Mexico State Forestry) has brought State Forestry, the FS, local governments, and private property owners together to address wildfire risks and the need to thin forests throughout this area. This funding mechanism has been essential in galvanizing efforts to create defensible space around and within communities as well as in creating opportunities to open up communication among the FS, other agencies, and homeowners.

Beneficial fire education programs stem from effective communication and acceptance of the protocols. A summary of suggestions for sound means of communicating fire information to the public includes focusing messages on the American public, in general, as well as on homeowners, specifically, and presenting messages in easily understandable lay terms. Both short-and long-term education programs are needed, such as the K through 12th grade program initiated by the Kaibab NF.

Others also recommend that more intense adult education efforts be implemented in the summer when both full-and part-time residents are present. An HOA member stated, "We make sure we have a meeting in the summer when most of the people are here." The local fire departments have asked neighbors to contact absent owners about clearing vacant lots. Residents said they find that homeowner meetings, flyers, door-to-door communication, and web sites are effective outreach tools. They also commented that printed material is more effective if pictures represent the regional ecosystem. Fire professionals discussed the importance of demonstration projects in visible areas to reach people concerning defensible space measures.

9.0 National Policy Experts Perspectives

Personal interviews were conducted with policy experts to provide a better understanding of current policy issues, how policy is developed, and how policies are implemented at the regional and local levels. The interviews were conducted either face-to-face or in conference calls between the researchers and the respective policy expert. Six interviews were conducted and the individuals were identified based on referrals from local, regional, and national experts. The following is a synopsis of the important themes that emerged from these conversations.

An overall theme that emerged, voiced by Kirk Rowdabaugh (Director, Office of Wildland Fire Coordination, US DOI, Washington, DC) was a statement of importance of social science research in understanding public wildland fire risk perceptions and the role those perceptions play in lay decisionmaking. He states that:

> We, as Program Managers, may have overestimated the value that citizens have put on their houses and underestimated the value they place on the landscapes around their homes. I think that social scientists could help us understand the way people evaluate risk. I'm interested in the sociological implications for our policies and whether or not we truly are taking into account the values of society, if we have that right or not. I think there are, of course, two different questions: one is how people make decisions—how they value risk—and then the other is what they value.

In addition, major themes and needs that were identified from our interviews included the development of a new wildland fire decision support system (WFDSS), improved means of coordination and communication among agencies, supporting communities in their fire prevention and management efforts, air quality and smoke management, and climate change/changing fire environments.

Tom Zimmerman (Program Manager for Wildland Fire Management Research Development and Application, USFS Rocky Mountain Research Station, Boise, Idaho) discussed his work in developing a WFDSS that will be an improvement over previous models. The WFDSS will promote better decisionmaking and will potentially lead to a greater ability to manage exponentially increasing fire suppression costs. According to Zimmerman, the Federal wildland management policy has now been revised to allow a single wildfire to be designated for the multiple objectives of resource benefit and protection—adaptive management that responds to a dynamic situation. In the past, a fire was managed for only one objective. The primacy of fire suppression is giving way to the realization of the multiple benefits that fire can provide. Wildland fires are now referred to as either "planned wildland fires" (prescribed burns) or "unplanned wildland fires." If an unplanned wildland fire occurs in an area where there has been authorization through land use plans to use fire to accomplish resource benefits, then it can be allowed to burn. If the fire occurs in an area with potential for damage to humans, structures, roads, etc., then the "protection objective" is invoked and suppression mechanisms are implemented.

Rowdabaugh also expressed that the primacy of suppression is being questioned. He states that as times change, agencies cannot continue to put every fire out, deferring risk to a later date. "One big change," he says, "is designating wildfire for resource benefit as well as suppression at the FS."

Improving coordination and communication among agencies involved in fire management was discussed by Rich Lasko (Assistant Director, USFS Fire and Fuels Ecology, Washington, DC) as well as by Rowdabaugh. Lasko mentioned the formal mechanisms of interagency coordination such as the Wildland Fire Leadership Council, the National Wildfire Coordinating Group (NWCG), the Fire Executive Council (FEC), and the Western Fire Leadership Coalition. He believes these groups are important because they bring together people who may be engaged with fire programs but not at the national implementation level. These groups are important in strategy and policy. The FEC represents the Fedeal leadership of fire management, the highest level in the agencies that deal with fire.

Improving communication among agencies and to the field, as well as reforming fire finance and budget development/formation, are also issues of concern. Rowdabaugh believes that communication across agencies is not perfect but that is not due to lack of effort. Interests of the interagency fire management programs and the specific agencies do not always line up, but in general, the interagency groups are able to work with agencies so that implementation at the field level is not impacted. He also stresses that decisionmaking should not only consider effects on Federal partner agencies but also on state, tribal, and local member groups. Lasko mentions the long chain of communication within the FS—he would like to see crisper, more direct communication that is in sync with the way information moves today and that is not based on writing a letter. "We've got to figure out a way to speed up our messages." However, he does feel that interagency communications are pretty good, considering the presence of two large bureaucracies (USDI agencies and the USDA FS), which may cause some time lag.

Several interviewees focused on the role and importance of providing assistance to communities in the form of money, education, training and assistance with Community Wildfire Protection Plans (CWPPs). Jim Hubbard (USFS Deputy Chief, State and Private Forestry, Washington, DC) described the role of State and Private Forestry in working with the 50 State Forestry organizations as the delivery agents to private landowners. According to Hubbard, assistance to landowners takes three forms: (1) annual grants to State Fire Assistance, (2) Fire Learning Networks, and (3) Firewise programs. The money comes from Washington, DC, and the states then allocate it where they believe it will be most effectively used. Donald Griego, Chief of Fire Management, New Mexico State Forestry, and Chairman of the SWCG, based out of Santa Fe, New Mexico, also described working with CWPPs to identify problem areas in the community plan and to rank what areas have the highest need for Federal funding. The SWCG spearheads interagency coordination among land management agencies in New Mexico, Arizona, and a portion of Texas focusing on wildland fire suppression and coordination of fuels treatments. The group acts as an interagency team that supports field units to complete projects. When the communities with the highest need are identified, the Forestry Division provides funding and prescriptions to communities to treat high fuel levels.

Coordinating between institutions is important because there are many gaps in coverage. Treatment on either Federal or private land does not help to protect the at-risk communities. Griego commented, "By us mandating that they work together…and complete the entire project to protect the whole community—I think that helps." The coordinating group also encourages people to introduce prescribed fire into the landscape to avoid catastrophic fires. In addition, Griego mentioned that New Mexico uses Firewise widely to educate communities. Rowdabaugh also stated that "how we're doing" in fire fuels (management) and community relations is one of his keen interests. He believes that State Foresters are the mechanism by which Federal partners are able to direct influence onto non-Federal properties. Lasko continued with thoughts on the importance of the interface with local communities. As he said:

> It's not just a fuels problem…. The other component is the community interface—how the community is prepared for fires. So the communities themselves have to be built in an appropriate way for the environment they live in. We're trying to develop a good picture of what needs to happen at those…levels and then how to integrate those to come up with a strategy, an appropriate strategy for the National Forest System.

Lasko continued by outlining his role as a Fire and Fuels Ecologist. According to him, the FS has good capabilities in the areas of fuels and preparedness, but needs work in the area of sustainability of structures in communities against fire. He feels that National FS fire professionals have a strong relationship with the FS research branch, but he would like to see more research on the effectiveness of fuels treatments and the longevity of that effectiveness. Specifically, he would like to see a methodology that would rate a site in terms of its effectiveness against fire—to determine whether or not the treatment has been successful.

In our interviews, we asked the experts to consider the topics of climate change and air quality/smoke management. Griego, Zimmerman, and Lasko discussed smoke management issues and implications for air quality. Griego mentioned that the EPA has come out with new smoke regulations so New Mexico Forestry Division and the Federal land management agencies must engage in meetings with the public to produce new guidelines. Without public input, projects could be restricted on State, private, or Federal lands. Zimmerman stated that smoke management, production, and air quality are not built in to the WFDSS model yet. "That's an area where we need to move quickly," he said. Zimmerman's group is interested in linking its part of the model to that of the Blue Sky Group in Seattle because there is much promising work to be done jointly. Lasko focuses on short-term conditions versus long-term conditions concerning air quality issues, stating that there is a need to display the effects of the FS Fire and Fuels Ecology work and program on those issues. He states that the FS should be looking at the impact of all fires on air quality as management decisions are made. Human health and safety must be considered in management decisions. According to Lasko, his group has been working with FS research to develop ways to monitor air quality conditions to give people the information they need to make better decisions. The air quality issues are significant right now and there are many political constraints. Lasko states, "What we need to do is be able to display those trade-offs (between short-term success and smoke) and then allow people to make decisions."

We had considerable interest in discussing the views of our informants concerning climate change and the possibility of changing fire environments. Not surprisingly, our most detailed discussion on the topic was provided by Allen Soloman, USFS National Program Leader for Global Change, Washington, DC. His work is focused on global climate change and its influence on management policies for forests. He believes Congress should fund an effort to develop an integrated assessment model on climate change because currently only "bits and pieces" are being studied. He also stated that there is funding for climate change proposals for Research Stations, but Station Directors are autonomous when it comes to prioritizing how to use their share of research dollars. According to Soloman, many of the research heads view climate change as a national problem, not their specific area problem, so they are not spending on climate change projects. Thus, according to Soloman, there is a need for an integrated assessment at the national level.

Soloman continued his discussion by stressing the importance of adaptive management under conditions of changing climate stating, "We are at the very beginning of integrating climate change into the management and maintenance of forest management." Griego also indicated that there has just been a "taste of climate change." He says that we are starting to see fires in areas that we haven't seen fires before—that we've just seen the tip of the iceberg so far.

Soloman argues for the need to educate people so that management actions such as thinning and prescribed fire can be understood and accepted. Managing forests for carbon storage is an appropriate management objective for healthy forests that are fire-resistant. Policymakers and stakeholders on the ground need to view forests as more than just a "stock of carbon" in Soloman's view. He advocates moving things out of the forest into long-life products or into biofuels to replace fossil fuels, leaving room for more carbon to be stored in a dynamic rather than a static system. He sees a growing belief among some stakeholder groups, such as the Sierra Club and Defenders of Wildlife, that active/adaptive management is important. Supporters of the Endangered Species Act must understand that removing some of the biomass in old growth stands is not going to conflict with management for the spotted owl, for example. These species, within their ecosystems, can all be managed together, according to Soloman.

Working at a more specific, localized level, Hubbard explains how selection of high priority treatment areas is being driven by climate change. In his opinion, there is a change in fuel conditions because of climate that goes beyond drought. Fuel moisture content is lower, the fire season is longer, temperatures are higher, and humidity is lower. He describes this as a long-term situation that will shift priorities for treatment because of season, fuel conditions, long-term effects, and insect/disease outbreaks that are closely tied to increased susceptibility from climate changes.

Tom Zimmerman discussed how climate change conditions are being incorporated indirectly into the previously mentioned WFDSS model. He explained how the effects of extended fire season are measured and tracked through the national fire danger rating system and weather forecasting. The effect of climate change on fuels, fuel moisture, local conditions, and fire behavior are reflected through the fire danger tracking, the fuel moisture monitoring, and the fire weather information used as inputs into the fire behavior model. Zimmerman continued that we need flexible policies to respond to dynamic conditions with the FS pushing to include climate change factors in modeling efforts. According to Zimmerman, there is no question that the fire environment is changing, resulting in dramatically rising fire suppression costs. He added that we may be setting new baseline data in terms of fire season length, fire season intensity, and duration of individual fires, among others. According to him, better documentation of these changes is needed because the current fire situation may not be one that can be better managed—it may be one that requires a different kind of

management or a different scale of management and budget. The better the information we have, the better the decision support system will be. Realization of the need for budget change at the Federal level is evident with the passage of the Federal Land Assistance, Management and Enhancement (FLAME) Act 2008.

Rowdabaugh also responded that climate change is one of the adaptive management challenges of the future, stating that fire management policies need to anticipate the likely consequences of a rapidly changing fire environment. According to Rowdabaugh, there are huge challenges at the Federal, State, Tribal, and local levels. As he said:

> *It is my hope, and the reason I actually sought this job, was to be able to participate in the development of appropriate policies to address those macro-changes in the fire environment (climate change, cyclical drought, overstocking and cross-management, insects and disease, demographic trends). All of that will translate into policies about how we address wildland fire, and how we manage vegetation, and how we partner with our non-Federal partners in and around the interface.*

He concluded, "If our policies fail to account for the likely consequences of climate change, then we will have failed completely."

These experts stressed the value of on-the-ground implementation of national-level policies and coordination efforts. The majority of these experts have served at various field levels in their agencies. They recognize the importance of work that is relevant to those implementing projects at the regional and local levels. In addition, the importance of interagency coordination and cooperation is a major concern of this group. They discussed the view that coordinated action among multiple agencies can overcome critical gaps that occur when projects are only undertaken on lands owned by one agency or individual rather than on a landscape basis. Several also mentioned that working with FS researchers, especially on developing criteria for assessing the effectiveness of fuels treatments and on monitoring air quality conditions related to both managed fires and wildfires, can be very helpful. All of the experts interviewed identified the necessity of integrating global climate change scenarios into adaptive forest and fire management policies, and all considered climate change the great management challenge of the coming years.

10.0 Possible Steps for the Forest Service

Interviews with communities, user groups, local government personnel, homeowners, and agency staff from the four forests across the region provide some valuable take-home messages for the FS. Many may seem obvious but are highlighted by the information we have received during this set of in-depth discussions and interviews with the various stakeholders on the four NFs as well as the regional survey of the general public.

The Santa Fe and Lincoln NFs demonstrate some of the problems faced by the agency in the region. Trust and communication are deemed to be lacking on the Santa Fe NF with members of the local communities. However, the relationship with local government officials and fire departments seems to be quite positive. When comparing this Forest to the Lincoln NF, it can be seen that the Santa Fe NF has a variety of factors leading to both historic and contemporary distrust, which complicate communication and fire education efforts. Many rural communities surrounding the Forest are resource-dependent and fear lost access to resources that have provided their livelihoods for generations. Resource-dependent portions of the other Forests (such as the southern portion of the Lincoln NF and portions of the Kaibab NF and Tonto NF) have the same problems and resulting distrust of agency actions and motivation.

Organized environmental groups are active on all the forests and seem to harbor distrust for the agency and for most resource-using groups across the board. Region 3 fire staff indicated that projects have been withdrawn because of litigation from environmental groups. Some fire management plans have been litigated, which stops wildland fire use because naturally ignited fires cannot be allowed to burn in certain areas without a management plan in place. Many of the major regional environmental groups are headquartered in Santa Fe and have a particular interest and focus on this Forest. Until recently, more remote areas have not been targeted so heavily. There is rising conflict among the resource users, the agency, and the environmental groups, which increases overall distrust. In addition, the Santa Fe NF is home to a vocal ethnic minority/majority that views itself as disenfranchised and robbed by the Government and the FS. Communication with this group is difficult, and the agency is perceived to be in the early stages of implementing the needed communication skills to work productively in this part of the region.

Interviews from the four Forests consistently stated that the constant movement of FS officials in and out of the area hampers communication and trust. Stakeholders feel unable to build up comfortable, trusting relationships with agency people. Many people told us of the importance of local, personal, direct contacts in their relationships with the agency. They value key, known FS employees who can help them to get things done. Respondents who are FS personnel said they believe that the number of people retiring from the FS is resulting in much institutional knowledge and talent leaving the agency, thereby increasing this "power void" in working with the community. The Region 3 Fire & Aviation management team believes that the "...pipeline is empty of experienced people and budgets are declining, which means that the agency lacks people with leadership, ability, risk assessment, and communication skills."

Those we spoke with recommend that the agency listen to the local people, respect their knowledge, and incorporate it into educational programs—not only to develop rapport with the people but also to improve the programs. Stakeholders across the board want to be respected, valued, and included in the decisionmaking process. They would like to see the days of the FS as "lone experts" end.

Homeowners and many others from all of the Forests desire solid, practical fire education programs that help them to not only mitigate fire risk to their properties but also to understand the role of fire in southwestern ecosystems. People want options, not dictatorial statements concerning what has to be done to their property. They seek education in plain, lay language.

Respondents from forests that have had recent, large wildfires recommended more coordination among fire-fighting and management agencies. They complained of not receiving enough specific information during the wildfire event. Some of these complaints concerning specific information during wildfire situations probably cannot be remedied. However, during the more normal times of prescribed fire and thinning projects, more information is perceived to be better than less information—no interviewee complained of receiving too much information. Many complained about a lack of information, an unclear decisionmaking processes, and perceived withholding of information. Residents would like to see the FS communicate more with the public and educate them on the effects and benefits of various treatments, among other things, as well as keep residents informed about what the agency is doing. For example, as one resident of the Santa Fe NF notes, "Probably 99 percent of prescribed fires accomplish their goals without any problem at all...so they need to get that type of information out to the public."

In addition, changes in wildfire policies by agencies around the world create a feeling of confusion and distrust among WUI residents everywhere. Fire staff from Region 3 echoed the importance of consistency within the agency and among agencies, stating that consistency is key because agency activities do not know boundaries between the regions. Although adaptation by agencies to changing conditions and new information and techniques are considered necessary and acceptable, consistent policies and communication within the agency and across agencies are desired by many stakeholders. The critical lesson is that all segments of the affected public understand that policies need to adapt to the dynamic nature of the on-the-ground conditions.

However, in order to accept and understand these changes, it is important that continuous communication strategies be used.[6]

A recent example is the changes in Australian fire policies for homeowners resulting from the 2009 Victoria bushfires, called "Black Sunday." The fires resulted in the death of 173 residents and the destruction of more than 2000 homes and structures. One result of the catastrophic bushfires was the investigation of the "Stay or Go Early" approach advocated for years by the Australian government. The commission found that many people did not receive warnings or were unaware of the threat to themselves and their property—the information necessary to make the policy effective. These findings resulted in a change in emphasis in the "Stay or Go Early" policy from staying and defending to leaving early with warnings that were based on a new fire danger index. At the highest fire danger level, the advice will be to leave rather than to stay and defend. The fire danger index is the basis for warnings and the associated community safety messages. The Australian Fire and Emergency Services Council has created a more sensitive fire danger index that links consistent national warning messages to the respective category on the fire danger index. The new messages will tell residents that the safest option is to leave when the index is over 100. (Handmer, November 2009).

Other things the FS can do to improve trust and communication include undertaking more treatment on public lands. As one resident of the Santa Fe area expresses, "There should be some new logging, there should be some more thinning in the forest and more controlled burns." While more logging is quite controversial, treatment of the urban interface is seen as the biggest priority and can be used to develop trust. Residents, such as a member of the Firewise Communities of Santa Fe, feel "[the FS is] going to have to help the homeowners, at least at this point, make a barrier between the forest and the communities."

Communicating effectively with FS personnel is sometimes seen as a challenge, but that challenge is often seen more on a national and regional level as opposed to the district level. People seem to have good working relationships with local district rangers once the rangers become known to the community, but they often find regional and district supervisors difficult to communicate with. There is acknowledgement of the challenge that the FS is faced with, as one Santa Fe resident states, the "diverse community out there that [makes it hard] to communicate effectively to all different types of groups." However, local rangers that interact and try to be part of the community they serve can be, as one fire management officer in the Santa Fe observes, "very effective because people get to know them and they can communicate better that way." This way, rangers experience more participation within the local community.

It is interesting to note that communication and education not only refers to public education but also to education of professionals within the agency. Region 3 fire staff discussed the importance of education for line officers, especially new ones coming into the area, concerning the role and importance of fire in the ecosystem and the risks that are inherent in any prescribed fire. They discussed the importance of understanding those risks, acceptable versus unacceptable, and the trade-off between not doing something or doing something with that risk. The agency tends to reward those who put out all fires and do not take the risk that a fire may get out of control. "I can tell you for a fact that I could have easily lost my job over a mistake of a prescribed fire, but yet the culture (of the agency) needs to change where we recognize that when you do take on fire management, you have got to be willing to recognize that you are going to have escapes [fires getting out of control].... Congress doesn't like to hear that, they think we should be able to live without escapes."

Concerning public education programs, both agency fire professionals and lay people consider the role and importance of communication and fire education critical. The notion of using teachable moments as means of increasing the impact of public fire education messages was stressed. Many feel that the public is more motivated and open to fire risk reduction messages immediately after a fire. However, this motivation tends to dwindle with the passage of time. Thus, using the immediate experience of the fire as a teachable moment can be very effective in encouraging people to take risk mitigation measures to protect themselves and their property. Another important concept related to dissemination of education information concerning fire risk mitigation activities is the idea that managers should tailor their education programs to the needs and knowledge levels of their varying stakeholder groups. These diverse groups of forest users and homeowners living in the WUI can include culturally, ethnically, and racially distinct groups, as well as those differentiated by age, education, income, and residential status (seasonal versus permanent). In addition to these factors, homeowners can be in varying stages of readiness to undertake risk reduction activities (Martin, Bender, and Raish 2007; Martin, Bender, and Raish 2008). Communicating risk vulnerability and severity, and effective means of remediating those risks, is critical. People must feel like they have the knowledge, ability, and resources to deal with identified risks and that the recommended actions will effectively reduce those risks.

Our research on fire risk reduction in the Southwest has shown that physically demonstrating what should be done, showing that assistance is available, and providing that assistance in a timely and reliable manner substantially increases feelings that risk reduction efforts can be accomplished (Martin, Bender, and Raish 2007; Martin, Bender, and Raish 2008). Direct, face-to-face communication in the form of presentations at local meetings and forest walks with locally knowledgeable people such as fire department

---

[6] Examples of continuous communication strategies include effective use of social media such as email lists, Facebook, blogs, etc. It is important to use a variety of communication strategies to keep all segments of the public informed of policy issues.

personnel are examples of effective forms of communication concerning risk reduction (Martin, Bender, and Raish 2007). Such educational efforts also have included developing demonstration plots that show what defensible space looks like and that include personalized property assessments to recommend what types of risk reduction activities should be undertaken by the property owner. Other activities include providing free pick-up and hauling, free or low-cost chipping, and burn pits for thinned materials. In some cases, Federal agencies and local communities have partnered to provide these services. Another valuable education technique is discussed by Mozumber and others (2009). They found that using wildfire risk maps can inform WUI residents of potential threats and can encourage risk reduction efforts. Providing wildfire risk maps to communities can also address policy goals by emphasizing information gathering and sharing among agencies and stakeholders to mitigate the effects of wildfires.

Different homeowner segments and user groups may also include distinct cultural, ethnic, and racial groups, which may require different educational techniques, methods, and hazard warnings. The literature on natural hazards response provides information on risk communication messages for both majority and minority populations, which can be useful for wildfire. Research has shown that differences exist in the ways in which minority and majority groups assess the credibility of hazard warnings and respond to those warnings. For all groups, however, sources must be considered credible and trustworthy before people will accept the message (Lindell and Perry 2004). Thus, it is important that managers know their affected stakeholders and who those people consider to be credible sources—respected community leaders or opinion leaders, for example. Research in the hazard literature has shown that peers are important in transmitting and influencing adoption of mitigation measures (Tierney 1994). Similarly, Lindell and Perry (2004) report that Hispanics were likely to consider friends, relatives, and neighbors as credible information sources, while whites and African Americans were less likely to consider these groups valid

sources of information. Various forms of the mass media can also be important for communicating hazard and risk information to the public. These forms of communication can be useful for managers in many instances. Using sources in an appropriate language for the audience is especially necessary when dealing with diverse ethnic groups. Language-specific television, radio stations, and newspapers can be helpful in this regard (Lindell and Perry 2004). Various researchers have found that different ethnic groups seem to prefer different media sources, with whites preferring print media, Hispanics preferring oral media such as local radio and television stations and neighborhood meetings, and African Americans preferring local radio, newspapers, and brochures from neighborhood meetings (Lindell and Perry 2004; Nelson and Perry 1991; Perry and Nelson 1991). It is also important that managers increase their own credibility by direct interaction and appropriate communication with their constituent groups, regardless of ethnicity (Lindell and Perry 2000, 2004, Lindell and Whitney 2000)[7].

This direct interaction with distinct user groups and homeowner segments allows managers to define and develop an understanding of the different stakeholder group leaders, needs, and communication preferences (Martin and others 2009). Many times, community leaders possess considerable valuable knowledge that can assist managers in working specific groups. In addition, observing the degree of risk-mitigating behaviors that have occurred among community subgroups can help the manager target appropriate risk communication strategies, taking into account the group's level of knowledge, motivation, and willingness to undertake further risk reduction activities. Research has shown that targeted, one-on-one information that is designed to address the issues of a particular property and physical characteristics of an area is more likely to move people to mitigate wildfire risks (Brenkert and others 2005) than general information in pamphlets and brochures. The underlying message for managers is that one size does not fit all when it comes to educational messages and techniques to encourage fire risk mitigation behaviors.

---

[7] Communication preferences could be changing based upon the increased availability of social media and online communication technologies.

11.0 Conclusions

Over a four-year period, we conducted a set of interviews with a broad set of stakeholders in four of the NFs in Region 3 (Santa Fe and Lincoln NFs in New Mexico and the Kaibab and Tonto NFs in Arizona). These interviews were the foundation for the second phase of the project—a survey of the general public surrounding the NFs within the Region. The final phase of the project was a set of interviews with national experts both in the FS and in other agencies. The information that was gathered was used to develop a picture of the fire risk beliefs and attitudes of individuals and groups within local communities; of local, regional, and national Government groups; and of special interest groups (for example, environmental, logging, and mining). The picture that emerged was one of commonalities across some dimensions and distinct differences across other dimensions. This information is designed to help local, regional, and National FS personnel to better understand the complexities of the risk beliefs and attitudes that guide how their stakeholder groups view the FS's role in the development and implementation of fire policies on public and private lands. As Kirk Rowdabaugh stated in his interview, the FS needs to develop a more in-depth understanding of the values that guide stakeholder perspectives on how both public and private lands are landscaped and fit together into a mosaic of ecosystems. He calls on social scientists, through research, to uncover the social values that guide how stakeholders make decisions about risks and how they value risks. The overall objective of this report is to do just that.

References

Brenkert, H.; Champ, P.; Flores, N. 2005. Mitigation of wildfire risk by homeowners. Res. Note RMRS-RN-25WWW. Fort Collins, CO: U.S. Department of Agriculture, FS, Rocky Mountain Research Station.

Condie, C.J. [Unpublished paper]. Documented uses of fire in prehistoric New Mexico. Unpublished paper on file at: U.S. Department of Agriculture, FS, Rocky Mountain Research Station, Albuquerque, NM.

Condie, C.J.; Raish, C. 2003. Indigenous and traditional use of fire in southwestern grassland, woodland and forest ecosystems. In: Jakes, Pamela J., comp. Homeowners, communities, and wildfire: science findings from the National Fire Plan. Proceedings of the Ninth International Symposium on Society and Resource Management; 2002 June 2-5; Bloomington, IN. Gen. Tech. Rep. NC-231. St. Paul, MN: U.S. Department of Agriculture, FS, North Central Research Station. 92 p.

Daniel, T.C.; Carroll, M.S.; Moseley, C.; Raish, C., eds. 2007. People, fire, and forests: a synthesis of wildfire social science. Corvallis, OR: Oregon State University Press. 226 p.

Dillman, D.A. 2000. Mail and internet surveys: The tailored design method, New York: John Wiley & Sons. 464 p.

Dobyns, H.F. 1981. From fire to flood. Ballena Press Anthropological Papers 20. Socorro, NM: Ballena Press.

Handmer, J. 2009, "Australian Fire Policy May Emphasize 'Go' over 'Stay and Defend'", Natural Hazards Observer, V. XXXIV(2), November.

Kay, C.E. 1994. Aboriginal overkill and native burning: implications for modern ecosystem management. Western Journal of Applied Forestry.

Lewis, H.T. 1973. Patterns of Indian burning in California: ecology and ethnohistory. Ballena Anthropological Papers Vol. 1. Ramona, CA: Ballena Press.

Lewis, H.Y. 1985. Why Indians burned: specific versus general reasons. In: Lotan, James E., et al. Tech. Co-ord. Proceedings: workshop on wilderness fire; 1983 November 15-18; Missoula, MT. Gen. Tech. Rep. INT-GTR-182. Ogden, UT: U.S. Department of Agriculture, FS, Intermountain Forest and Range Experiment Station:75-80.

Lindell, M.K.; Perry, R.W. 2000. Household adjustment to earthquake hazard: a review of research. Environment and Behavior. 32: 590-630.

Lindell, M.K.; Perry, R.W. 2004. Communicating environmental risk in multiethnic communities. Thousand Oaks, CA: Sage Publications.

Lindell, M.K.; Whitney, D.J. 2000. Correlates of seismic hazard adjustment adoption. Risk Analysis. 20: 13-25.

Martin, I.M.; Bender, H.W.; Raish, C. 2007. What motivates individuals to protect themselves from risk: the case of wildland fire. Risk Analysis. 24(4): 887-900.

Martin, I.M.; Bender, H.W.; Raish, C. 2008a. Making the decision to mitigate risk. In: Martin, WE.; Raish, C.; Kent, B. eds. Wildfire risk: human perceptions and management implications. Washington, DC: Resources for the Future Press:117-141.

Martin, W.E.; Brajer, V.; Zeller, K. 2008b. Valuing the health effects of a prescribed fire. In:Martin, W. E.; Raish, C.; Kent, B., eds. Wildfire risk: human perceptions and management implications. Washington, DC: Resources for the Future Press:244-263.

Martin, W.E.; Raish, C.; Kent, B. eds. 2008c. Wildfire risk: human perceptions and management implications. Washington, DC: Resources for the Future Press. 310 p.

Martin, W.E.; Martin, I.M.; Kent, B. 2009. The role of risk perceptions in the risk mitigation process: the case of wildfire in high risk communities. Journal of Environmental Management. 91(2): 489-498. DOI: 10.1016/j.jenvman. 2009.09.007.

Mozumber, P.; Helton, R.; Berrens, R. 2009. Provision of a wildfire risk map: informing residents in the wildland urban interface. Risk Analysis. 29(11): 1588-1600.

Nelson, L.; Perry, R.W. 1991. Organizing public education for technological emergencies. Disaster Management. 4: 21-26.

Perry, R.W.; Nelson, L. 1991. Ethnicity and hazard information dissemination. Environmental Management. 15: 581-587.

Pyne, S.J. 1982. Fire in America: a cultural history of wildland and rural fire. Princeton, NJ: Princeton University Press.

Pyne, S.J. 1995. World fire: the culture of fire on earth. New York, NY: Henry Holt.

Stewart, O.C. 1995a. Forest and grass burning in the Mountain West. Southwestern Lore. 21(1): 5-9.

Stewart, O.C. 1995b. Why were the prairies treeless? Southwestern Lore. 20(4): 59-64.

Tierney, K.J. 1994. Emergency preparedness and response. In: Practical lessons from the Loma Prieta earthquake. Washington, DC: National Academy Press:105-128.

Tierney, K.J.; Lindell, M.K.; Perry, R.W. 2001. Facing the unexpected: disaster preparedness and response in the United States. Washington, DC: John Henry Press.

Williams, G.W. 2002. Aboriginal use of fire: are there any "natural" communities? Washington, DC: U.S. Department of Agriculture, FS, Research Summary.

Winter, P.L.; Cvetkovich, G.T. 2008. Diversity in southwesterners' views of FS fire management. In: Martin, W.E.; Raish, C.; Kent, B., eds. Wildfire risk: human perceptions and management implications. Washington, DC: Resources for the Future Press:56-170.

Appendix A. Interview Guide

1. Some **background** on who we are and what we are doing with the FS. Use the information from the one-page summary of "Fire and Fuels Management" stressing the three major areas of interest in the focus group (issues, treatment options, wildfire risk levels and role of the FS, homeowner, local fire dept. etc.). Ask for permission to record the session. Explain to the person that we will use the transcripts to make sure the comments are accurately represented. Stress that we are interested in accurately representing their positions and opinions!

2. Ask each of the participants to **briefly introduce** themselves. For example, try to determine how long each individual has worked in wildfire, what is their background, wildfire experiences in other areas, memberships in any collaborative efforts, what their position is within the organization, etc.

3. Ask each individual how they are involved with the **management and use** of public lands. As information regarding the individual's relationship to public lands is discussed begin questioning them regarding **issues related to fire and fuels management**. Use the list of issues from the 'Issue Books' for each location to make sure that all issues are addressed. **Focus on their role as a decision maker or policy person.**

ISSUE LIST _____
_____
_____
_____
_____
_____
_____
_____
_____
_____
_____
_____

4. Once the discussion of the issues is complete ask them to identify their **objectives regarding fire and fuels management** in general and regarding their area specifically. Refer to the issue list to encourage discussion of objectives that may be related to the various issues.

5. Next, ask their **beliefs** about the 'role of the FS and their agency/affiliation' in fire and fuels management. Be sure to get as much context for their opinion as possible. Also, make sure to ask the individual

   - what they believe is the appropriate 'balance' between local versus national input, (be sure to address controversy regarding local knowledge/expertise; role of incident team; volunteer fire depts., etc.)
   - their belief as to the FS management structure and local autonomy, i.e. how much control should the Forest Supervisor have, the District Ranger?
   - what role should the Washington office have v. the region v. the forest v. the district?
   - At what level should wildfire policy be made? What input from others outside the agency is appropriate?
   - How is communication between the FS and other groups before a fire? During a fire? After a fire?

6. Probe to explore the link between climate change and wildfire management decisions.

   - Is there a link between wildfire and climate change?
   - Is climate change something they are required to address in their management efforts?
   - Do they believe there is enough evidence of a link to justify including climate change considerations in management decisions? **What do they believe versus what do they have to do!**
   - Is there enough evidence of a link to make it feasible to consider climate change in their decisions?
   - Do they have adequate access to scientific studies regarding the link between wildfire and climate change?
   - What is the primary source of information regarding this link?
   - Do they believe it is reliable—good science?
   - Is the public requesting that they consider climate change or is it internally driven or both?

7. Finally, ask if the individual has any questions about what we are doing. Thank them for their time and input. Let them know when we will be in contact and how they can contact us. Ask if they have any recommendations for others to talk to.

Appendix B. Survey to the General Public

A Survey on
Wildfire Management Issues Related
To Homeowners and National Forest Lands

Integrated Resource Solutions, LLC
1109 Four Mile Canyon Drive
Boulder, Colorado 80302

September 15, 2006

CIRCLE THE NUMBER THAT BEST FITS HOW YOU FEEL ABOUT EACH OF THE STATEMENTS:

A) Forest Treatment Options Related to Wildfire
The use of active fire management tools on National Forests includes prescribed fires, mechanical removal (thinning and logging), and others.

1. How effective is *prescribed or managed fire* at reducing the risks of wildfire:

1	2	3	4	5	6	7
not at all effective						very effective

2. How effective is *managing naturally ignited wildfires* at reducing the risks of wildfire:

1	2	3	4	5	6	7
not at all effective						very effective

3. How effective is *selectively thinning small diameter trees* (less than 16 inches in diameter) at reducing the risks of wildfire:

1	2	3	4	5	6	7
not at all effective						very effective

4. How effective is *selectively logging large diameter trees* (over 16 inches in diameter) at reducing the risks of wildfire:

1	2	3	4	5	6	7
not at all effective						very effective

5. How effective is *prescribed fire and thinning small trees in combination* at reducing the risks of wildfire:

1	2	3	4	5	6	7
not at all effective						very effective

6. How effective is *prescribed fire and logging large trees in combination* at reducing the risks of wildfire:

1	2	3	4	5	6	7
not at all effective						very effective

7. How effective is using *goats to reduce the amount of brush and vegetation* at reducing the risks of wildfire:

1	2	3	4	5	6	7
not at all effective						very effective

CIRCLE THE NUMBER THAT BEST FITS HOW YOU FEEL ABOUT EACH OF THE STATEMENTS:

8. How effective is *salvage logging* (removing burned trees after a wildfire) at reducing the risks of wildfire:

1	2	3	4	5	6	7
not at all effective						very effective

9. How effective is *thinning and logging infested or diseased trees* (removing dead or dying trees) at reducing the risks of wildfire:

1	2	3	4	5	6	7
not at all effective						very effective

10. How effective is *no active fire management* ("let nature take its course") at reducing wildfire risks:

1	2	3	4	5	6	7
not at all effective						very effective

11. Of the treatment options listed in questions 1-10, please list the <u>three</u> treatment options that you *prefer* to see land managers use to reduce the risks of wildfire.

1. _____

2. _____

3. _____

Please rate the following forest treatment statements:

1. Forest treatment options to reduce the risks of wildfire should be focused around communities.

1	2	3	4	5	6	7
strongly disagree						strongly agree

2. Forest treatments to reduce the risks of wildfire should be implemented across the entire national forests (for example, in the backcountry and around communities).

1	2	3	4	5	6	7
strongly disagree						strongly agree

3. Prescribed fire should only be used once the usable wood material is removed through commercial logging.

1	2	3	4	5	6	7
strongly disagree						strongly agree

USDA Forest Service RMRS-GTR-260. 2011.

CIRCLE THE NUMBER THAT BEST FITS HOW YOU FEEL ABOUT EACH OF THE STATEMENTS:

4. Prescribed fire should only be used once the usable wood material is removed through thinning (for example, fuel wood gathering, small-scale timber operations).

1	2	3	4	5	6	7
strongly disagree						strongly agree

5. If lives and structures are not threatened, the US FS should let wildfires burn as needed.

1	2	3	4	5	6	7
strongly disagree						strongly agree

6. Prescribed fire should **not** be used as a treatment because of the potential health (e.g. respiratory) problems from smoke.

1	2	3	4	5	6	7
strongly disagree						strongly agree

B) Effectiveness of the Current US FS at Managing Public Lands for the Risk of Wildfire

1. How effective is the <u>current</u> US FS at managing public lands to reduce the risk of wildfire:

1	2	3	4	5	6	7
not at all effective						very effective

2. How effective is the <u>current</u> US FS at implementing mechanical removal programs (for example, commercial logging) on national forest lands:

1	2	3	4	5	6	7
not at all effective						very effective

3. How effective is the <u>current</u> US FS at implementing thinning projects (for example, for fuel wood and small scale logging operations) on national forest lands:

1	2	3	4	5	6	7
not at all effective						very effective

4. How effective is the <u>current</u> US FS at implementing prescribed or managed fire programs on national forest lands:

1	2	3	4	5	6	7
not at all effective						very effective

CIRCLE THE NUMBER THAT BEST FITS HOW YOU FEEL ABOUT EACH OF THE STATEMENTS:

C)   Wildfires in the Wildland-Urban Interface

1. How vulnerable do you feel about the possibility of a wildfire physically affecting you or your family:

1	2	3	4	5	6	7
not at all vulnerable						extremely vulnerable

2. How vulnerable do you feel about the possibility of a wildfire affecting your property and/or possessions:

1	2	3	4	5	6	7
not at all vulnerable						extremely vulnerable

3. What is the perceived likelihood of wildfire happening near your home within the next couple of years:

0	1	2	3	4	5	6	7	8	9	10
No chance		probably will not happen			50-50 chance		probably will happen			certain to happen

4. On a scale of 0 to 10, how severe will the impact of a catastrophic wildfire be where you live:

0	1	2	3	4	5	6	7	8	9	10
no harm at all										extremely devastating

D) Responsibility of Various Groups in Safeguarding Lives, Property, and Lands

1. How responsible should **homeowners** be for protecting themselves and their property from the impact of wildfire:

1	2	3	4	5	6	7
not at all responsible						very responsible

2. How responsible should **homeowners' associations** be for protecting homeowners and private property from the impact of wildfire:

1	2	3	4	5	6	7
not at all responsible						very responsible

3. How responsible should **local governments (for example, county and city)** be for protecting homeowners and private property from the impact of wildfire:

1	2	3	4	5	6	7
not at all responsible						very responsible

CIRCLE THE NUMBER THAT BEST FITS HOW YOU FEEL ABOUT EACH OF THE STATEMENTS:

4. How responsible should the **US FS** be for protecting homeowners and private property from the impact of wildfire:

1	2	3	4	5	6	7
not at all responsible						very responsible

E) Residents' Knowledge and Experience with Wildfire

1. How well informed do you consider yourself to be about wildfire and wildfire risks:

1	2	3	4	5	6	7
not at all informed						very informed

2. To what extent do you find information about wildfires to be personally relevant?

1	2	3	4	5	6	7
not at all relevant						very relevant

3. How motivated are you to learn more about the connection between wildfire risks and undertaking the actions to make my property more defensible against wildfire:

1	2	3	4	5	6	7
not at all motivated						very motivated

4. What type of experience have you had with large-scale wildfire(s): Check all that apply.

____ My house and/or structures on my property were destroyed (partially or totally)
____ There have been fires very near my property (less than 5 miles)
____ There have been fires 5 to 50 miles from my property
____ There have been fires 51 to 100 miles from my property
____ I\we have been evacuated from my\our house because of the threat of a wildfire.
____ I\we have heard about wildfire experiences through friends, family or neighbors.
____ No experience
____ Other—please explain: _____

5. Have you received any information about wildfire risks from the following sources in the last year? Please check each source that has provided you wildfire information. Check all that apply:

____ U.S. FS (e.g. Firewise Community info, educational brochures)
____ Other Federal land management agencies (BLM, Park Service, etc.)   ____ State Forestry
____ County/City Fire Department
____ Local and State Law Enforcement
____ Media reports (TV, newspaper, radio)
____ Neighbors and/or friends
____ Environmental Organizations
____ Other (please specify._____)

WRITE THE NUMBER THAT BEST FITS HOW YOU FEEL ABOUT EACH OF THE STATEMENTS:

For each source checked above, how helpful was the information on a scale from *1=not at all helpful* to *7=very helpful*. If you do not have any experience with a group, please leave it blank.

6. <u>Information Source</u>   <u>How helpful?</u>

   U.S. FS (Firewise Community info, educational brochures)   _____

   Other federal agencies (BLM, Park Service, etc.)   _____

   State Forestry   _____

   County/City Fire Department   _____

   Local and State Law Enforcement   _____

   Media reports (TV, newspaper, radio)   _____

   Neighbors and/or friends   _____

   Environmental Organizations   _____

   Other (please specify_____)

Sections F, G, and H apply <u>only</u> to those homeowners who live or have property close to National Forest lands. Otherwise, you should go directly to Section I of the survey on page XX.

In the next section, we are interested in knowing what types of defensible space actions you and your family have taken on your property. Check the answer that best fits with what you have done on your property.

F) Defensible Space Actions on Private Property

1. What is your likelihood of doing the following actions to your property:

   a.   Creating a minimum 30-foot defensible space around your home:
        _____ Already done
        _____ Will do in next month
        _____ Will do in next 3-6 months
        _____ Will do next year
        _____ Probably will not do (Why not? _____)

   b.   Planting low-growing, fire resistant plants around your home:
        _____ Already done
        _____ Will do in next month
        _____ Will do in next 3-6 months
        _____ Will do next year
        _____ Probably will not do (Why not? _____)

   c.   Putting a fire resistant roof on your home:
        _____ Already done
        _____ Will do in next month
        _____ Will do in next 3-6 months
        _____ Will do next year
        _____ Probably will not do (Why not? _____)

   d.   Putting fire resistant undersides to any decks and balconies on your home:
        _____ Already done
        _____ Will do in next month
        _____ Will do in next 3-6 months
        _____ Will do next year
        _____ Probably will not do (Why not? _____)

CHECK THE CHOICE THAT BEST FITS WHAT YOU HAVE DONE OR INTEND TO DO:

e.   Removing any dead branches from your home's roof and around the chimney:
_____ Already done
_____ Will do in next month
_____ Will do in next 3-6 months
_____ Will do next year
_____ Probably will not do (Why not? _____)

f.   Making sure that your home is easily identifiable and accessible from a main road by emergency vehicles:
_____ Already done
_____ Will do in next month
_____ Will do in next 3-6 months
_____ Will do next year
_____ Probably will not do (Why not? _____)

g.   Making sure that all the trees on your property are planted away from structures :
_____ Already done
_____ Will do in next month
_____ Will do in next 3-6 months
_____ Will do next year
_____ Probably will not do (Why not? _____)

h.   Making sure that all the trees on your property are planted away from overhead utility lines:
_____ Already done
_____ Will do in next month
_____ Will do in next 3-6 months
_____ Will do next year
_____ Probably will not do (Why not? _____)

i.   Working with neighbors to prune and clear common areas with heavy vegetation:
_____ Already done
_____ Will do in next month
_____ Will do in next 3-6 months
_____ Will do next year
_____ Probably will not do (Why not? _____)

j.   Stacking firewood and scrap wood piles at least 30 feet from any structure:
_____ Already done
_____ Will do in next month
_____ Will do in next 3-6 months
_____ Will do next year
_____ Probably will not do (Why not? _____)

k.   Contacting your local fire department to get a personal fire safety inspection oft your home and property:
_____ Already done
_____ Will do in next month
_____ Will do in next 3-6 months
_____ Will do next year
_____ Probably will not do (Why not? _____)

G) Effectiveness of Risk Reduction Actions

How effective are the following actions at reducing the risk of wildfire from impacting your property and lives. Using the scale below, insert an X in the column that best fits with how effective you believe each action is at reducing the risk of wildfire.

1	2	3	4	5	6	7
Not at all Effective						Very Effective

		1	2	3	4	5	6	7
a.	Create a 30-foot defensible space around your home:							
b.	Plant low-growing, fire resistant plants around your home:							
c.	Put a fire resistant roof on your home:							
d.	Putting fire resistant undersides to any decks & balconies on your home:							
e.	Removing any dead branches from your home's roof and around the chimney:							
f.	Making sure that your home is easily identifiable and accessible from a main road:							
g.	Making sure that all trees on your property are planted away from structures:							
h.	Making sure that all the trees on your property are planted away from overhead utility lines:							
i.	Working with neighbors to prune and clear heavy vegetation on common areas:							
j.	Stacking firewood and scrap wood piles at least 30 feet away from any structure:							
k.	Contacting the local fire department to get a fire safety inspection at your home:							

4. By doing any of the above actions on your property, **how effective can you be at** preventing wildfires from impacting your personal property and your life:

1	2	3	4	5	6	7
not at all effective						very effective

5. How **confident do you feel in your ability** to protect your property and yourself from the risk of wildfire:

1	2	3	4	5	6	7
not at all confident						very confident

USDA Forest Service RMRS-GTR-260. 2011.

H) Confidence in Ability to Undertake Defensive Actions

How confident do you feel in your ability to conduct any of these defensible actions on your property in an effort to reduce the risks of wildfire impacting you and your property. Using the scale below, insert an X in the column that best fits with how confident you feel in your ability to undertake each of these actions in an effort to reduce the risk of wildfire.

1	2	3	4	5	6	7
Not at all Confident						Very Confident

		1	2	3	4	5	6	7
a.	Create a 30-foot defensible space around your home:							
b.	Plant low-growing, fire resistant plants around your home:							
c.	Put a fire resistant roof on your home:							
d.	Putting fire resistant undersides to any decks & balconies on your home:							
e.	Removing any dead branches from your home's roof and around the chimney:							
f.	Making sure that your home is easily identifiable and accessible from a main road:							
g.	Making sure that all trees on your property are planted away from structures:							
h.	Making sure that all the trees on your property are planted away from overhead utility lines:							
i.	Working with neighbors to prune and clear heavy vegetation on common areas:							
j.	Stacking firewood and scrap wood piles at least 30 feet away from any structure:							
k.	Contacting the local fire department to get a fire safety inspection at you or home and property:							

2. What would you say is the biggest impediment or constraint to taking some action to protect your property from the impact of wildfire? Please specify:

3. What convinced you to take defensible space action on your property? Please check all that apply.

_____ Major fire event
_____ Suggestions by local government (for example, local fire department)
_____ Suggestions by federal government
_____ Insurance incentive
_____ Aesthetics
_____ Creating a healthy forest

_____ Improving wildlife habitat
_____ Getting rid of dead or dying trees (for example, from bug infestations)
_____ Reducing wildfire risks
_____ Have not taken any action
_____ Other—please explain: _____

I) For the following questions, please check the appropriate category or fill in the appropriate information.

1. Where is your **primary residence**: _____
(city and state)

2. Please identify your age group:

18-25 _____	45-54 _____
26-34 _____	55-64 _____
35-44 _____	65 and over ___

3. Please identify your gender: _____ Male   _____ Female

4. What is your highest level of education completed:

Some high school _____	High School _____
Some college _____	College degree _____
Postgraduate work _____	Graduate degree _____
Other (please specify _____)	

5. If you have <u>a home near the forest</u>, how many months per year do you live in your home near the forest: _____ # of months

6. If you have <u>a home near the forest</u>, how close is your **home** to the closest National Forest or Grassland?

_____ less than 1 mile	_____ 21 to 50 miles
_____ 1 to 10 miles	_____ more than 50 miles
_____ 11 to 20 miles	_____ Other (please specify _____)

7. Please check the category which best fits your household income level per year:

Less than $15,000 _____	$35,000 – $49,999 _____
$15,000 – $24,999 _____	$50,000 – 74,999 _____
$25,000 – $34,999 _____	$75,000 – over _____

8. Please identify the zip code for your **primary residence**: _____

9. Please identify the zip code for your **residence near the forest**: _____

10. With which racial/ethnic group do you most closely identify?

11.

_____ African American/Black	_____ Mexican American
_____ Central American	_____ Native American/First Nation (Please
_____ Chinese American	Specify: Nation/Tribe/Pueblo_____
_____ Cuban American	_____)
_____ Hispanic American	_____ Vietnamese American
_____ Japanese American	_____ White American/Caucasian
_____ Korean American	_____ Other Ethnic/Racial Group (Please
	Specify:_____)

10a. Please mark the appropriate statement concerning Hispanic or Latino ethnicity:

_____ Hispanic or Latino   _____ Not Hispanic or Latino

12. If you were born outside the US, how many years have you lived in the US? _____ (# of years)

13. What is the **primary** language you speak at home?

English _____   Spanish _____   Other (please specify) _____

14. How many times have you visited National Forests in the past 12 months?

THANK YOU FOR YOUR PARTICIPATION!

If you have any questions or comments about the survey or topics related to what was covered in this survey, you are welcome to put that information in this section. If you would like us to respond to any questions that you may have please include your name and address/contact email so that we can respond.

Appendix C. Survey of General Population— Results

Forest treatment options related to wildfire:

The use of active fire management tools on National Forests in the western United States includes prescribed fires, mechanical removal, and other techniques. We asked residents of Arizona and New Mexico (FS Region 3) to rate the effectiveness of 10 different forest treatment strategies to help reduce the risk of devastating wildfires (1 = not at all effective to 7 = very effective). The 10 strategies considered are:

1. prescribed or managed fire,
2. managing naturally ignited wildfires,
3. selectively thinning small-diameter trees,
4. selectively logging large-diameter trees,
5. prescribed fire and thinning small-diameter trees in combination,
6. prescribed fire and thinning large-diameter trees in combination,
7. using goats to reduce the amount of brush and vegetation,
8. salvage logging,
9. thinning and logging infested or diseased trees, and
10. no active fire management.

The results of these effectiveness measures are presented in table 1. The results are presented for the entire region and then by each of the four targeted areas.

The results in table 1 provide information on how effective all respondents perceived the 10 treatment options to be as tools to mitigate the risks of catastrophic wildfire. Overall, the results show that doing nothing to mitigate wildfire risks is not perceived as a desirable option by the public. This is also apparent when looking at the means by location. What is interesting is that for the most part, there was a consistent perception of how effective each of these treatment options are across all four sites.

Table 1. Effectiveness ratings of forest treatment options.

Forest treatment options preferences	Overall mean (SD)	Arizona		New Mexico	
		northern region	southern region	northern region	southern region
Prescribed fire	4.86 (1.50)	4.81 (1.55)	5.11 (1.19)	4.66 (1.51)	4.90 (1.70)
Managing naturally ignited fire	4.34 (1.47)	4.42 (1.44)	4.38 (1.46)	4.20 (1.52)	4.37 (1.52)
Selective thinning— (small wood)	5.11 (1.42)	4.85 (1.56)	5.02 (1.34)	5.30 (1.37)	5.33 (1.33)
Selective thinning— (large wood)	4.21 (1.73)	4.07 (1.71)	4.31 (1.68)	4.30 (1.75)	4.21 (1.86)
Prescribed fire and thinning small wood	5.18 (1.44)	5.09 (1.54)	5.46 (1.22)	5.15 (1.44)	5.03 (1.52)
Prescribed fire and logging	4.43 (1.74)	4.38 (1.73)	4.75 (1.76)	4.43 (1.63)	4.10 (1.85)
Goats	4.75 (1.69)	4.63 (1.55)	4.49 (1.81)	5.01 (1.67)	4.92 (1.79)
Salvage logging	4.69 (1.78)	4.50 (1.92)	4.67 (1,69)	4.74 (1.74)	4.96 (1.74)
Thin diseased trees	5.55 (1.54)	5.52 (1.64)	5.54 (1.22)	5.61 (1.51)	5.58 (1.48)
Do nothing	2.08 (1.45)	2.41 (1.69)	1.81 (1.24)	1.83 (1.05)	2.32 (1.66)
Sample size	502	152	119	141	90

USDA Forest Service RMRS-GTR-260. 2011.

Three most preferred defensible space actions:

We also asked the respondents to rank their top three treatment options/strategies. They were asked to list the three treatment options that they preferred to see public land managers use to reduce the risks of wildfires. Table 2 lists the three most preferred options by all four locations as well as for the entire sample.

What emerges from this analysis is that overall, respondents prefer treatment options that do not involve the use of prescribed fire. If you look at the top three choices across the four sites, it is evident that selective thinning, salvage logging, and thinning diseased/infested trees were consistently preferred. The one exception was that the use of goats as a means to reduce brush and vegetation was found to be preferred by New Mexican respondents. Another interesting point that emerges is that selectively logging large-diameter trees was not preferred by any site along with the option of doing nothing. It should be noted that these preferences were listed without considering the cost to implement the various treatment options.

Table 2. Preferred treatment options.

Treatment option	All locations	Arizona		New Mexico	
		northern region	southern region	northern region	southern region
Most preferred treatment option	Selectively thinning small-diameter trees	Selectively thinning small-diameter trees	Selectively thinning small-diameter trees and diseased trees (salvage logging)	Selectively thinning small-diameter trees	Selectively thinning small-diameter trees
Second most preferred treatment option	Salvage logging and using goats	Thinning and logging diseased trees	Salvage logging	Goats to reduce brush and vegetation	Goats to reduce brush and vegetation
Third most preferred treatment option	Thinning and logging diseased trees	Salvage logging	Thinning and logging diseased trees	Thinning and logging diseased trees	Thinning and logging diseased trees

Where and what should be the focus of the various forest treatments:

Not only were we interested in what types of forest treatment options were preferred and how effective all the various treatment strategies were perceived to be by respondents, but we also wanted to know where these forest treatment options should be focused in an effort to reduce the risks of wildfire. Respondents were asked to rate their level of agreement with two statements that said "Forest treatments options to reduce the risks of wildfire should be focused around communities/should be implemented across the entire National Forests." They were then asked to rate their level of agreement with "Prescribed fires should only be used once the usable wood material is removed through commercial logging/removed through thinning projects." Then they rated their level of agreement with the statement "If lives and structures are not threatened, the U.S. Forest Service should let wildfires burn as needed." Finally, they were asked to rate the statement "Prescribed fires should not be used as a treatment because of the potential health problems from smoke." These six statements were designed to provide more in-depth explanation for respondents preferences as they relate to the various treatment options and strategies (1 = strongly disagree to 7 = strongly agree). Table 3 provides the means and standard deviations for this set of questions.

One result of these questions was the preference that forest treatments should focus on the entire National Forest, including wilderness areas, as well as areas around communities using these treatments. We also found that respondents felt that if prescribed fire is going to be used, all the usable wood material should be removed through some form of thinning such as fuel wood gathering, small-scale timber operations, etc. This is consistent with the results in table 1 and table 2. Surprisingly though, respondents were not concerned with the potential health issues that often result from smoke due to wildfires and prescribed fires.

Table 3. Forest treatment preferences.

Forest treatment preferences	Overall mean (SD)	Arizona		New Mexico	
		northern region	southern region	northern region	southern region
Focus on communities	5.22 (1.52)	5.28 (1.52)	5.10 (1.56)	5.33 (1.48)	5.12 (1.55)
Focus across entire Forest landscape	4.97 (1.85)	4.59 (1.94)	5.39 (1.81)	5.23 (1.66)	4.69 (1.92)
Use fire after commercial logging	4.63 (2.05)	4.46 (1.99)	5.39 (1.81)	5.23 (1.66)	4.69 (1.92)
Use fire after thinning projects	5.22 (1.66)	5.09 (1.60)	5.26 (1.76)	5.50 (1.55)	4.92 (1.77)
Let it burn unless lives are threatened	4.13 (1.91)	4.24 (1.69)	3.78 (2.04)	4.16 (1.94)	4.36 (2.00)
No prescribed fire if smoke is health problem	3.18 (1.74)	3.16 (1.71)	3.07 (1.71)	3.23 (1.78)	3.31 (1.84)
Sample size	502	152	119	141	90

FS management practices:

The next set of questions were focused on evaluating the effectiveness of current U.S. FS practices at managing public lands for the risk of wildfires (1 = not at all effective to 7 = very effective). Respondents were asked to rate how effective the current U.S. FS is at managing public lands to reduce the risk of fire, implementing commercial logging programs, implementing thinning projects, and implementing prescribed fire programs on National Forest lands.

The results in table 4 illustrate that respondents have a neutral evaluation of the effectiveness of these policies. This could be due to their lack of knowledge about the effectiveness of U.S. FS management policies or about how to determine the effectiveness.

Table 4. Effectiveness of various forest management practices.

| Effectiveness | Overall mean (SD) | Arizona | | New Mexico | |
		northern region	southern region	northern region	southern region
Current management practices	4.08 (1.25)	3.93 (1.30)	4.04 (1.03)	4.25 (1.31)	4.13 (1.35)
Current mechanical removal	3.94 (1.33)	3.89 (1.40)	3.65 (1.25)	4.16 (1.34)	4.06 (1.24)
Current thinning projects	3.87 (1.27)	3.91 (1.25)	3.49 (1.17)	3.96 (1.31)	4.18 (1.30)
Current prescribed fire projects	3.87 (1.34)	3.81 (1.43)	3.81 (1.05)	3.99 (1.34)	3.87 (1.51)
Sample size	502	152	119	141	90

Wildfires in the WUI:

In order to get a clear understanding of how residents in the WUI feel about their safety, we asked them to rate their feeling of vulnerability to the risk of wildfire for themselves and their house and property (1= not at all vulnerable to 7 = extremely vulnerable). We also asked them what their perceived likelihood was of a wildfire happening near their property and how severe they would expect that wildfire to be (0 = no chance/no harm at all to 10 = certain to happen/extremely devastating). Table 5 presents the results for Arizona and New Mexico as well as by location.

In table 5, the low to moderate perceptions of the wildfire risks emerged across all four locations. When asked about their feelings of vulnerability, respondents seemed to believe that the possibility of wildfires affecting them and their property was moderate. Their belief that a catastrophic wildfire could happen near their property was low for southern Arizona and moderate for the other three regions. It is possible that this perception is due to the ecology and the topography of the region. The Sonoran Desert portions of southern Arizona are not adapted to fire and generally have lower fire risk than higher-elevation forested areas. Finally, when asked how severe the impact of a wildfire would be within the next couple of years, again, the southern region of Arizona was significantly lower than the other three locations.

Table 5. Perceived vulnerability, risk likelihood, and severity of potential wildfires.

| Perceived vulnerability | Overall mean (SD) | Arizona | | New Mexico | |
		northern region	southern region	northern region	southern region
How vulnerable are you?[a]	3.33 (1.96)	3.66 (1.95)	2.68 (1.75)	3.45 (2.03)	3.49 (2.01)
How vulnerable is your home?[a]	3.24 (2.05)	3.58 (2.05)	2.56 (1.91)	3.37 (2.13)	3.44 (1.99)
Likelihood of wildfire[b]	3.51 (2.69)	4.13 (2.72)	2.62 (2.62)	3.67 (2.64)	3.36 (2.58)
Severity of wildfire[b]	5.02 (3.25)	5.27 (3.15)	3.91 (2.94)	5.42 (3.43)	5.38 (3.33)
Sample size	502	152	119	141	90

[a] These measures are based upon a 7-point scale.
[b] These measures are based upon a 0 to 10 rating.

Responsibility of various groups in safeguarding lives, property, and lands:

Another important factor in understanding the public's perception of how to mitigate wildfire risks is to understand where the public places responsibilities for this mitigation process. We asked the public how responsible should individual homeowners, homeowner's associations, local governments, and the U.S. FS be (1 = not at all responsible to 7 = very responsible). The responses to these questions continue to help us construct a picture of how residents in the WUI view the process of mitigating wildfire risks for all parties concerned (see table 6).

The responsibility for protecting oneself, property, and lands is another issue that has been found to determine what homeowners will do to mitigate wildfire risks. The results indicate that across all locations, respondents believe strongly that homeowners are responsible for protecting themselves and their property. Likewise, they believed that HOAs should also be held responsible for protecting homeowners and private property. This could be due to the issue that occurs when some homeowners do little or nothing to mitigate fire risks on their property, resulting in a potentially negative spillover effect on others in the community. Next, respondents also believe that county and city governments along with the public land managers are responsible for working to mitigate wildfire risks. All in all, the overarching belief is that mitigating wildfire risks is the responsibility of all members of the community, including the FS.

Table 6. Responsibility for protecting against wildfires.

Responsibility	Overall mean (SD)	Arizona		New Mexico	
		northern region	southern region	northern region	southern region
Homeowners' responsibility	6.36 (0.94)	6.35 (0.98)	6.43 (0.93)	6.40 (0.88)	6.24 (1.01)
HOA's responsibility	5.83 (1.43)	5.75 (1.45)	6.09 (1.30)	5.67 (1.63)	5.89 (1.21)
Local government responsibility	5.59 (1.52)	5.57 (1.39)	5.62 (1.54)	5.65 (1.55)	5.50 (1.70)
U.S. FS responsibility	5.27 (1.56)	5.11 (1.55)	5.31 (1.59)	5.37 (1.56)	5.31 (1.60)
Sample size	502	152	119	141	90

Residents' knowledge of and experience with wildfire:

Next, we measured how much information and experience respondents had with wildfires. We asked how informed they were about wildfire risks, how personally relevant they found information on wildfires, and how motivated they were to learn as much as possible about wildfires (1 = not at all informed/relevant/motivated to 7 = very informed/relevant/motivated). We also asked them what type of experience they had with large-scale wildfires including such aspects as being evacuated, losing homes or structures, etc. Finally, they were asked to report what type of information that they had been exposed to over the last year related to wildfires. Sources of information included Federal, state, and local agencies, media reports, neighbors, environmental organizations, and fire departments. The results to these questions are presented in table 7.

Overall, respondents believed that they were moderately well-informed and motivated to learn more about the connection between wildfire risks and defensible space actions. This was also consistently true in each of the four locations. In addition, respondents felt that information about wildfires was moderately relevant to them, providing an opportunity to further inform residents in these two states.

Table 7. How informed and motivated are WUI residents?

Knowledge	Overall mean (SD)	Arizona		New Mexico	
		northern region	southern region	northern region	southern region
How well-informed	4.77 (1.52)	4.61 (1.46)	4.75 (1.56)	4.84 (1.55)	4.96 (1.56)
How relevant is information	4.65 (1.58)	4.69 (1.48)	4.38 (1.68)	4.79 (1.62)	4.71 (1.54)
How motivated to learn	4.78 (1.68)	4.76 (1.68)	4.38 (1.71)	4.93 (1.64)	5.15 (1.66)
Sample size	502	152	119	141	90

Defensible space actions on private property:

To determine how respondents used the knowledge and information that they had to mitigate wildfire risks on their properties, we asked them to tell us what their likelihood was of undertaking 11 defensible space actions[1]:

1. creating a 30-foot defensible space around your home,
2. planting fire-resistant plants around your home,
3. putting a fire-resistant roof on your home,
4. putting fire-resistant undersides to decks and balconies,
5. removing dead branches from roof,
6. making sure home is easily identifiable from main road,
7. making sure all trees are planted away from structure,
8. making sure all trees are planted away from utility lines,
9. working with neighbors to prune and clear common areas,
10. stacking firewood away from structures, and
11. contacting local fire department for a personal fire safety inspection.

The response options for each item were: 1 = already done, 2 = will do in next month, 3 = will do in next 3–6 months, 4 = will do next year, and 5 = probably will not do (0 = not applicable). Table 8 provides the frequencies for each option at each location and for the entire sample.

The southern part of Arizona had significantly fewer defensible space actions undertaken by respondents. In fact, southern Arizona residents are in sharp contrast to the other three sites when it comes to 7 of the 11 risk mitigating actions. For the defensible space action of "working with neighbors to clear common areas," southern Arizona and southern New Mexico were both significantly less likely to undertake this action. In addition, they also had a significant number of respondents state that they would not undertake this action, unlike the northern regions of both New Mexico and Arizona. When looking at the defensible action of "stacking wood away from structures," we found that a number of residents in both southern Arizona and northern New Mexico would not undertake this action (20% and 25%, respectively), while southern Arizona was significantly more likely to have undertaken this action (45.5%). Another interesting result was for the action of "planting trees away from utility lines," southern New Mexico was the only site where a significant percent stated that they would not do this defensible action (55%). Finally, for the defensible space action of "having a fire safety inspection," we found that there was much variation across locations. About 25% of respondents in three of the four locations had already undertaken this action while about 25% said they would not do it (southern Arizona and both sites in New Mexico). In contrast, 50% of respondents in northern Arizona had already undertaken the action while 30% would not consider taking this action. Overall, there was some variation in 3 of the 11 defensible space actions, but for the other 8, there was a consistent pattern, as previously described.

Table 8. Defensible space actions taken.

Defensible space action	Overall mean	Arizona		New Mexico	
		northern region	southern region	northern region	southern region
30-foot defensible space	58% already done	64% done already	47.2% already done	65.3% already done	50% already done
Plant fire resistant plants	56% already done	61.8% already done	38.2% already done	53.5% already done	72.5% already done
Fire resistant roof	62% already done	66.3% already done	47.3% already done	73.5% already done	50% already done
Fire resistant undersides	55% will not do	64.1% will not do	35.2% will not do	45.3% will not do	79% will not do
Remove dead branches	81% already done	77.2% already done	67.3% already done	92.3% already done	90% already done
Easily identify house	83% already done	93.3% already done	63.6% already done	83.8% already done	85% already done
Trees planted away from house	62% already done	66% already done	52.7% already done	63.4% already done	60% already done
Trees planted away from utility lines	63% already done	72.8% already done	52.7% already done	71.8% already done	55% will not do
Work with neighbors	48% already done	57.6% already done	42% already done and 33% will not do	49.3% already done	55.3% will not do and 34.2% already done
Stack firewood away	63% already done	68% already done	45.5% already done & 20% will not do	62.8% already done & 25% will not do	68.5% already done
Fire safety inspection	34% already done and 32% will not do 48.9% already	done & 37% will not do	21.8% already done & 21.8% will not do	28% already done, 21% will do in next 3–6 months, & 24% will not do	30% already done & 45% will not do
Sample size	502	152	119	141	90

Effectiveness of risk reduction actions:

We then asked respondents to tell us how effective each of the risk reduction actions are (1 = not at all effective to 7 = very effective). We also asked respondents, by doing these defensible space actions, how effective would they be at preventing wildfires from impacting their property and their lives (1 = not at all effective to 7 = very effective). We then asked them to rate how effective these types of defensible space actions are at preventing wildfires from impacting their personal property and their lives (1 = not at all effective to 7 = very effective). The results to all these behavior measures are presented in table 9.

The pattern of how effective each of the defensible space actions were perceived to be was very consistent across all four locations for all 11 actions. For the most part, respondents felt that these actions were effective at reducing the risk of wildfires damaging property or injuring individuals. The overall rating of how effective these defensible space actions are was very high.

Table 9. Effectiveness of the risk reduction actions.

| Defensible space action | Overall mean (SD) | Arizona | | New Mexico | |
		northern region	southern region	northern region	southern region
30-foot defensible space	5.31 (2.03)	5.32 (2.06)	5.28 (2.14)	5.37 (1.87)	5.16 (2.23)
Plant fire resistant plants	5.20 (1.76)	5.36 (1.82)	5.21 (1.41)	4.97 (1.75)	5.26 (2.02)
Fire resistant roof	5.93 (1.54)	6.10 (1.59)	6.17 (0.99)	5.88 (1.56)	5.65 (1.89)
Fire resistant undersides	5.12 (2.04)	5.01 (2.16)	5.55 (1.67)	5.19 (1.86)	4.81 (2.44)
Remove dead branches	6.15 (1.40)	5.94 (1.56)	6.33 (1.28)	6.24 (1.37)	6.24 (1.14)
Easily identify house	5.94 (1.38)	5.97 (1.41)	5.95 (1.10)	5.89 (1.53)	6.00 (1.31)
Trees planted away from house	5.41 (1.81)	5.32 (1.88)	5.38 (1.77)	5.53 (1.66)	5.39 (2.04)
Trees planted away from utility lines	5.28 (1.97)	4.97 (2.07)	5.69 (1.73)	5.49 (1.89)	5.13 (2.35)
Work with neighbors	5.10 (2.12)	4.82 (2.07)	5.47 (2.06)	5.23 (1.89)	5.11 (2.37)
Stack firewood away	5.97 (1.69)	5.74 (1.97)	6.21 (1.34)	6.14 (1.42)	5.89 (1.81)
Fire safety inspection	5.23 (1.79)	5.41 (1.83)	5.28 (1.56)	4.90 (1.84)	5.42 (1.83)
Overall effectiveness	6.00 (1.28)	5.96 (1.37)	6.12 (1.15)	5.92 (1.29)	6.02 (1.25)
Sample size	502	152	119	141	90

Confidence in ability to undertake defensible space actions:

It is also important to understand what affects a person's decision to either undertake or not undertake these 11 defensible actions. Related to the factors that influence the decision to undertake the defensible space action is a person's respective confidence in their ability to undertake these defensible actions. These tasks can require considerable physical effort and can be very costly to implement. Therefore, we measured respondents' confidence levels at undertaking each of the defensible actions as well as their overall confidence in their ability to protect themselves and their property (1 = not at all confident to 7 = very confident). The results to all these behavior measures are presented in table 10.

The same pattern emerged for the degree of confidence that respondents had in their ability to undertake these defensible actions except for three types of actions. The first is putting fire-resistant undersides to decks and balconies on a home. This could be because some residents did not have balconies and decks, so this was not perceived as relevant to their situation. The second action was planting trees away from houses and structures. The reasoning for this lower confidence level could be that many people are not willing to cut down trees close to their structures or do not intend to plant more trees. The third action was working with neighbors to clear common areas. This could be due to the lack of organized HOAs or other community organizations. The overall level of confidence in undertaking defensible space actions was moderately high for all locations.

Table 10. Confidence in ability to undertake defensible actions.

Defensible space action	Overall mean (SD)	Arizona		New Mexico	
		northern region	southern region	northern region	southern region
30-foot defensible space	5.17 (2.35)	5.62 (2.16)	4.58 (2.15)	5.30 (2.15)	4.47 (2.65)
Plant fire resistant plants	5.71 (1.79)	5.88 (1.74)	5.61 (1.98)	5.62 (1.72)	5.63 (1.86)
Fire resistant roof	5.79 (1.92)	6.20 (1.46)	5.25 (2.30)	5.87 (1.97)	5.26 (2.10)
Fire resistant undersides	4.75 (2.48)	5.31 (2.27)	4.75 (2.57)	4.59 (2.46)	3.73 (2.60)
Remove dead branches	6.30 (1.31)	6.54 (0.92)	5.95 (1.86)	6.27 (1.42)	6.20 (0.94)
Easily identify house	6.35 (1.29)	6.53 (0.97)	5.90 (1.93)	6.58 (0.95)	5.94 (1.45)
Trees planted away from house	4.98 (2.33)	5.13 (2.23)	4.90 (2.41)	5.10 (2.30)	4.54 (2.52)
Trees planted away from utility lines	5.17 (2.47)	5.35 (2.35)	5.32 (2.53)	5.35 (2.37)	4.08 (2.71)
Work with neighbors	4.82 (2.32)	5.07 (2.03)	4.91 (2.44)	4.75 (2.39)	4.21 (2.60)
Stack firewood away	6.05 (1.79)	6.13 (1.77)	5.98 (1.93)	6.26 (1.42)	5.47 (2.17)
Fire safety inspection	5.72 (1.72)	5.83 (1.64)	5.60 (2.04)	5.72 (1.69)	5.59 (1.55)
Overall confidence	5.72 (1.20)	5.78 (1.22)	5.98 (1.32)	5.56 (1.04)	5.54 (1.26)
Sample size	502	152	119	141	90

Demographic characteristics of WUI residents:

The last section of the survey focused on a set of demographic questions, and the results are presented in Table 11. Respondents were asked to select the category of demographic variables that best described their household. This included some individual-level variables such as age and gender as well as some household-level variables such as race/ethnic group. These variables were used to develop a description of the typical household in each of the four regions of New Mexico and Arizona. The household-level variables were measured based upon the census category of occupied housing since the survey was of home addresses. Table 12 provides a comparison of the survey sample to Arizona and New Mexico averages for the main demographic variables.

Table 11. Demographic characteristics.

		Arizona		New Mexico	
Age	**Overall**	**northern region**	**southern region**	**northern region**	**southern region**
18–25	4%	1%	1%	1%	1%
26–34	7%	2%	2%	1%	2%
35–44	15%	4%	4%	4%	3%
45–54	30%	9%	7%	8%	6%
55–64	21%	6%	65	6%	3%
65 and over	23%	8%	4%	7%	4%

		Arizona		New Mexico	
Gender	**Overall**	**northern region**	**southern region**	**northern region**	**southern region**
Male	68%	22%	18%	17%	12%
Female	32%	8%	6%	11%	6%

		Arizona		New Mexico	
Education	**Overall**	**northern region**	**southern region**	**northern region**	**southern region**
Some high school	0.5%	0	0.25%	0.25%	0
High school graduate	19%	4%	7%	5%	3%
Some college	12%	5%	0	3%	4%
College degree	29%	9%	4%	11%	6%
Postgraduate work	17%	6%	3%	6%	2%
Graduate degree	21%	4%	7%	9%	2%

		Arizona		New Mexico	
How close is home to forest lands	**Overall**	**northern region**	**southern region**	**northern region**	**southern region**
Less than 1 mile	24%	10%	2%	8%	4%
1 to 10 miles	33%	10%	6%	10%	8%
11 to 20 miles	22%	7%	2%	8%	5%
21 to 50 miles	12%	5%	5%	3%	1%
More than 50 miles	7%	3%	2%	1%	1%

		Arizona		New Mexico	
Income	**Overall**	**northern region**	**southern region**	**northern region**	**southern region**
Less than $15,000	3%	1%	1%	1%	0
$15,000–$24,999	8%	2%	1%	3%	2%
$25,000–$34,999	10%	3%	2%	3%	3%
$35,000–$49,999	23%	7%	4%	8%	4%
$50,000–$74,999	20%	6%	5%	5%	4%
$75,000–over	35%	11%	11%	7%	6%

		Arizona		New Mexico	
Racial or ethnic group	**Overall**	**northern region**	**southern region**	**northern region**	**southern region**
African American	1%	0.25%	0	0.25%	0
Hispanic American	14%	4%	1%	6%	3%
Asian American	1%	1%	0	0	0
Native American	1%	0	0	1%	0
White/Caucasian	84%	26%	23%	21%	15%
Sample size	502	152	119	141	90

Table 12. Sample and state comparisons.

Age	Sample	Arizona	New Mexico
< 35	11%	22%	22%
35–44	15%	19%	18%
45–54	30%	20%	21%
55–64	21%	17%	18%
>65	23%	22%	21%

Gender*	Sample	Arizona	New Mexico
Male	68%	50%	50%
Female	32%	50%	50%

*Because we surveyed households, the gender distribution is skewed toward male respondents.

Education	Sample	Arizona	New Mexico
Some high school	1%	14%	16%
High school graduate	19%	23%	25%
Some college	12%	35%	32%
College graduate	67%	29%	27%

Racial or ethnic group*	Sample	Arizona	New Mexico
African American	1%	3%	2%
Hispanic American	14%	21%	39%
Asian American	1%	2%	1%
Native American	1%	3%	7%
White/Caucasian	84%	83%	75%

*Columns may not total to 100% due to overlap between Hispanic and White self-identification.

Income	Sample	Arizona	New Mexico
< $15,000	3%	12%	16%
$15,000–$24,999	8%	11%	13%
$25,000–$34,999	10%	11%	12%
$35,000–$49,999	23%	16%	15%
$50,000–$74,999	20%	19%	18%
>$75,000	35%	31%	26%

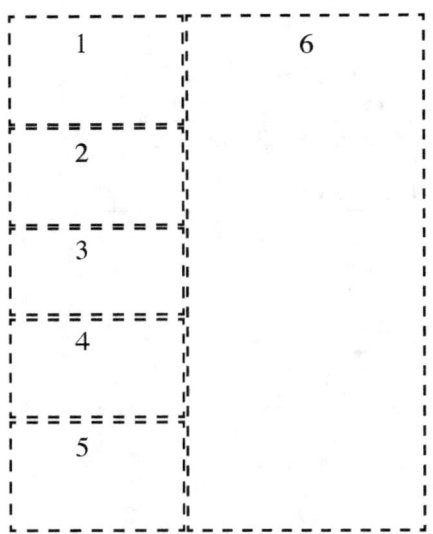